D0308793

Tony Geraghty was born in Liverpool in 1932 and grew up in wartime London as a 'blitz kid'. After military service as a sergeant with 16th Independent Parachute Brigade Group in Cyprus and Egypt in the 1950s, he started a career in journalism. He joined the *Sunday Times* as chief reporter in 1968 and his assignments then took him to the world's trouble spots, including Nigeria, Syria and Jordan, eastern Europe and Northern Ireland. In 1979 he became defence correspondent and specialized in irregular warfare studies. Tony Geraghty is now a freelance author and journalist. His bestselling postwar history of the SAS, *Who Dares Wins,* is also available in Fontana.

This is the
SAS

A pictorial history of the
Special Air Service Regiment

TONY GERAGHTY

FONTANA/COLLINS

First published by Arms and Armour Press, Lionel Leventhal Ltd
1982
First issued in Fontana Paperbacks 1983

Copyright © Tony Geraghty 1982
Copyright © Lionel Leventhal Ltd 1982

Designed by David Gibbons and edited by Tessa Rose
Typeset by Typesetters (Birmingham) Ltd
Made and printed in Great Britain by
William Collins Sons & Co. Ltd, Glasgow

△3 ▽4

1. A volunteer for 23 SAS (TA) crossing the Brecon Beacons in
1981.
2–4. The SAS has always been rich in characters. Men such as
'The Frontiersman' (**2**), armed here with a 7.62mm Lee Enfield
Sniper rifle and, over his shoulder, an M79 grenade-launcher;
'The Ditch' (**3**); and 'The Monk' (**4**). Dhofar.

Inside cover illustrations
(Front) Top left: Wet jump into the sea by Boat Troop soldiers from
RAF Hercules (SAS Regiment). Top right: Dressed for mountain
warfare, Dhofar, Oman, 1972: the 'Ditch' (Bruce Niven). Below left:
Wrecked Pucara, Pebble Island (SAS Regiment). Below right: The
price of heroism: the grave of Captain John Hamilton (posthumous
MC) on West Falkland, 1982 (SAS Regiment).
(Back) Top: Contact in Borneo and the hunt is up (SAS Regiment).
Below: Launching the Gemini in heavy surf: Boat Troop begins a
rough ride (SAS Regiment).

 **Contents**

6 Introduction

8 North Africa, 1941—1943
The desert raiders

18 Aegean and Adriatic, 1943—1944
'Yarnder loom the islands'

28 Italy and North-West Europe, 1943—1944
Partisans v. Panzers

40 Malaya, 1950—1959
'Boots, boots moving up and down again'

54 Jebel Akhdar, Aden and Borneo, 1959—1967
Minimum force

68 Dhofar, 1970—1976
Persuasion and firepower

84 Contemporary Conflict, 1969—
The dirty war

102 Selection and training
The long hard road

116 Exercises
Risk without glory

128 Ritual (and other tribal customs)

134 The Australians
Special forces unlimited

138 The New Zealanders
In at the beginning

145 The Falklands
A synthesis of things past

Introduction

This book is an essay in photographic history and its subject is the Special Air Service Regiment. Like its predecessor, *Who Dares Wins*, this work makes no special claim to be definitive, though nothing known to the author has been deliberately excluded or distorted. Unlike *Who Dares Wins*, it attempts to include in its coverage the major activities of the Regiment during the Second World War, and it approaches its subject through the photographic record rather than the written word.

Such an approach has the same disadvantage as television journalism — 'The pictures are wonderful, old boy, so let's get them in somehow' — but this shortcoming, hopefully, is offset by the verisimilitude of the camera in capturing the moment. That technique was one which Henri Cartier-Bresson, the French photographic master, raised to a form of art, sometimes gracefully but sometimes to shocking effect, as in his print of an aged priest, followed by an even more aged peasant woman, averting their eyes from two dogs enthusiastically copulating in a village square. Such moments are created by the 'Cosmic Joker'. Cartier-Bresson in his exhibitions presents these moments for what they are: startling images with no coherent connection with what went before or after.

The historian is more arrogant. He plays God and says, in effect: 'This is how it was'. Official historians, concerned with continuing political sensitivities, sometimes cheat in the process. One of the best documented cases of the photographic record (though not the camera) being obliged to lie in the interests of realpolitik concerns the place of the Soviet pioneer Leon Trotsky in the history of the USSR. When the Stalinist régime decided to rewrite history, it had to eliminate the all-too-visible contribution of the man whom it had murdered in exile. So the censor's brush simply painted Trotsky out of group photographs of modern Russia's founding fathers which included Stalin and Lenin. It is to the credit of those who have advised the author about the security aspects of this book that they have sought to paint out no one. This is as well, for the faces in these pages matter far more than any of the author's words.

But, if this book is neither a 'definitive' history nor a random collection of frozen moments, what is it? As an essay, it tries to reconstruct what was *typical* of any given period in the history of the SAS. It endeavours to capture the flavour·of the soldier's life on special operations in the Aegean, in Borneo, Oman, or wherever. Much — probably most — of that life is spent in monkish hard living and boredom, a stark and basic business of keeping the body nourished, mind alert and weapons in working order. As a way of life, it is now as remote from that of most people in modern society as the Romans'. It is also one that teaches even the most arrogant young warrior a proper stillness and humility, as well as scepticism.

The moments of action, when they occur, are larger than life: witness the photographs published here for the first time of terrified hostages fleeing to safety from their hijacked aircraft in Mogadishu; the ambush scenes in Borneo; the military sky-diving sequences, and so on. To sustain repeated exposure to a life pattern of hardship/boredom/explosive action requires a very special, controlled personality. Outsiders, including critics of the SAS, believe that this results from some sort of sinister brainwashing. Uncritical admirers of the Regiment believe that its soldiers are supermen. Both views are wrong. SAS soldiers are tested almost to destruction if they stay with the Regiment long enough, and they learn to develop their own inner resources of strength, optimism, humility and humour on the job, just as other adventurous spirits do elsewhere. It is to those soldiers, most of them non-commissioned officers, that this book is dedicated.

In essence, the personality of the SAS has not changed during the forty years described in these pages. What has changed is the nature of the enemy and the methods by which people now make war on one another. Until the 1960s, the SAS fought other combatants who were, fundamentally, full-time soldiers on battlefields from which most civilians had been removed. The seventies have seen the creation by extremists of every political persuasion of a potential battlefield in virtually every part of the civilized world. As a result of a real or imagined collective injustice, such extremists claim a licence to kill, imprison and mutilate people totally uninvolved in their private quarrel. Such extremists, and their apologists in universities, the communications media, the legal profession and mainstream politics have made atrocities a norm of political protest.

The SAS, which has probably saved more lives than it has taken during its existence — through direct medical care, by cutting short otherwise prolonged military engagements, and (as in Borneo) through the skilled application of minimum force — has responded to the terrorist threat with patience as well as cunning and skill at arms. The first two qualities are peculiarly necessary in an armed force that is subject to the rule of law rather than the law of the jungle. SAS soldiers are answerable to society in a way in which terrorists, who by nature are fascist as well as élitist, are not. So it is in the soldiers' interests, as well as those of society at large, that we should understand slightly better what sort of people they are and what they are trying to achieve. Such is the condition of the modern world that understanding is now necessary, because we all potentially share the battlefield with them. The process of understanding is not assisted by excessive and unnecessary secrecy.

As this book was nearing completion, the regimental compass pointed south and the clock turned back. In April 1982, the Argentine invasion of the Falkland Islands and the suppression of British freedom there was swiftly followed by the sudden absence of SAS soldiers from their customary haunts in Britain. Such enigmatic disappearances had occurred before, many times; so often as to be a cliché of SAS life. What made this operation different was the number apparently involved.

The tasks facing those involved were a test even of SAS versatility. Virtually no-one in the Regiment had previous experience of Antarctica, the South Atlantic or Latin America, though the men of 'G' Squadron had kept intact skiing, climbing and other Arctic warfare skills on long, punishing treks in Norway. In the harsh British winter that had just ended, others had taken to skis and lived in snow-holes in the Welsh mountains, in temperatures of around minus 25° Centigrade, for recreation.

The environment within which the South Atlantic conflict was to be fought was not only cold, it was also largely an amphibious one. It would be reasonable, therefore, to suppose that the Boat Troop men would come into their own. In fact, the available evidence points less to the use of submarine-launched Gemini inflatables and scuba-diving techniques than to the audacious employment of helicopters. Flown cunningly, these machines can be put down with remarkably little noise. As a result of such tactics, SAS ferret parties were creeping round Argentine garrisons to assess their strength long before the main British landing at San Carlos anchorage.

Working with the SAS were the more modest number of men available from the Royal Marine Commando Special Boat Section. The SBS shares much with the SAS including a crowded period of its history, as the section of this book devoted to SAS/SBS activities in the Aegean indicates. Both organizations, ultimately, are the offspring of Bob Laycock's 8 Commando. And both, historically, place as much emphasis upon intelligence as military muscle. The first SBS commander, Roger Courtney, decorated his office with a notice proclaiming: 'Are you tough? If so, get out! I need buggers with brains.'

After the war the SBS was taken over by the Royal Marines. It is a miniscule part of that corps, and its members are only considered for selection after completing basic Royal Marine training, followed by a commando selection course, service with one of the fighting units and, in most cases, further specialized training in the Arctic warfare and mountaineering cadre.

SAS Boat Troop soliders and SBS commandos have much in common. Their training and techniques — as the training section of this book reveals — are similar. It is probably fair to say that SBS men have the edge over their SAS colleagues in long distance, underwater scuba-diving, and the navigational problems this creates. The essential difference is one of role. SBS men are concerned primarily with methods of entry into hostile territory from the sea, rivers, fjords and canals. They might accomplish this by the simple, wartime expedient of posing as fishermen on surface craft. Equally, they can parachute into the sea already wearing wet suits and flippers. Once inshore they might be expected to acquire data on everything from coastal radar to the depth of water near possible landing sites for the invasion force that is to follow them.

They might also await the arrival of such a force, calling it in by coded radio or torch. If there is to be a commando raid then they are the hand that guides the raid rather than the spearhead of it. If the task is to put Allied agents ashore in hostile territory or to find and recover them, then the SBS would be expected to be 'tip-toe boys', unseen and unheard. In that sense they are the maritime equivalent of the war-time Long Range Desert Group. Their offensive role is what it always has been: attacks on enemy shipping and harbour installations. They are probably the world's most expert troops in underwater demolition. In recent years their skills have been employed in defending Britain's North Sea oil rigs against possible terrorist assault. Here they must practise the appallingly risky art of rendering harmless submerged explosive devices attached to the rigs.

The SAS, by contrast, was conceived by David Stirling as a long range, *strategic* force that would penetrate deep into enemy territory for months at a time rather than days or weeks, and once there, demolish targets inaccessible to the RAF or anyone else. Modern communications and target-designation devices, such as laser illuminators, enhance the SAS capability for destruction by proxy, through the use of air or artillery strikes.

In the South Atlantic, as at other times, the military problem did not match the niceties of military theory. On a few occasions it has been necessary for the SAS to operate in larger formations as a result. It is already clear that in the South Atlantic the SAS operated in greater strength than at any time since those brief periods of the Dhofar campaign in Oman when two squadrons were in action simultaneously in the same theatre. The prizes were great: recovery of South Georgia, and with it Britain's stake in Antarctica; a brilliant raid on Pebble Island in the Falklands, resulting in the destruction of a greater number of Argentine aircraft than in any of the air battles; raids on other occupied areas including Goose Green; the acquisition of invaluable intelligence by the ferret parties. Some of these operations are described in more detail in the Falklands section of this book.

The Regiment's losses reflected the scale of its success and the inevitable risk. In a catastrophic accident involving one Sea King helicopter, eighteen SAS men were lost. They included veterans whose experience was irreplaceable: two sergeant-majors, one staff-sergeant and four sergeants. The number of fatalities in this single incident was greater than anything the Regiment had suffered since Operation 'Loyton' in Occupied France on 18 June 1944, when an entire troop of seventeen men was lost in an aircraft accident. Proportionately, the loss was much greater in 1982, for in 1944 the SAS had many more soldiers. In its usual, stoic way the SAS tribe closed ranks after its losses off the Falklands. But in a letter to the Defence Ministry, an SAS widow wrote: 'I wish to pay my deepest respect to my husband who gave me so much support and understanding, and I hope that the courage he showed will help sustain me in the years ahead.' An SAS soldier, asked how he felt, replied simply, 'Just angry.'

Tony Geraghty, 1982

North Africa, 1941-1943
The desert raiders

5. The man who started it all: David Stirling, in his desert days. An early ally, David Lloyd-Owen of the Long Range Desert Group, said of him: 'There was never a more convincing talker than Stirling once he had an idea in his head. On top of this, he had a burning passion to fight the enemy and unbounded confidence that given surprise he would always be able to destroy them, despite the odds with which he might be faced . . . Failure meant nothing more to him than to generate fierce determination to be successful next time.' Less solemnly, John Lodwick of the SBS wrote: 'David Stirling was the military Marks & Spencer. Like some vast organization of chain stores his force grew . . . and kept growing, nourished by success, fortified by prestige and an intriguing aura of mystery.'

From its inception, the Special Air Service Regiment has believed that small is elegant and cost-effective, provided that the lack of number is balanced by quality. In 1941, when the SAS was created by David Stirling and his comrades, other commando forces already existed. These were born from the aggressive vision of Winston Churchill who, after the fall of France in 1940, wanted to demonstrate that the British Army was not a spent force. But these other commandos, brave and highly trained as they were, suffered from several disadvantages. They mounted brief, intensive raids on a large scale, usually against well-defended targets, and suffered heavy casualties as a result. They required ships of the Royal Navy to put them ashore and, more critically, to bring them out again.

Stirling's idea, drafted in pencil from a hospital bed in Cairo, was that four-man patrols parachuted behind enemy lines and capable of getting themselves home (eventually) could create havoc by attacking airfields, harbours, petrol dumps, railways, telephone lines and road convoys. At the time, Stirling was a Scots Guards lieutenant serving with No. 8 Commando, which was part of a 3,000-strong brigade drafted to the Middle East to make amphibious raids against Nazi-occupied Mediterranean ports and islands. This group, known as 'Layforce', launched some daring operations, including a raid on Rommel's headquarters. But an amphibious force needs ships and, as time passed, none was available. 'Layforce' was disbanded.

Stirling found himself in hospital after injuring his back while making the first, experimental descent of a 'Teach Yourself Parachuting' course. His friend 'Jock' Lewis, an Oxford rowing blue, had mysteriously acquired a batch of military parachutes, and these two, with four others, had decided to try them out from the bomb bay of an ancient Valentia aircraft. Stirling's canopy had snagged the aircraft tail and had not given him much support after that. He is a big man and the baked Egyptian desert makes for hard landings. Initially, the injury paralysed his legs.

With characteristic cheek, Stirling, a junior officer, climbed into the defended headquarters of the general commanding Middle East forces, General Claude Auchinleck, and delivered his proposal in person. He was rewarded with promotion to captain and given permission to raise something called 'L' detachment of a non-existent Special Air Service Brigade. The nomenclature was intended to deceive. Far from a brigade, the authorized strength of the new unit was 66 commandos of the dismembered 'Layforce'. Of these, 53 took part in the first disastrous parachute operation on 16 November 1941. The drop was made in darkness and stormy conditions, and 32 were killed or taken prisoner. The SAS licked its wounds, recruited more men and re-thought its tactics. The outcome was a working partnership with the Long Range Desert Group, which would assist the SAS in reaching its targets behind the lines and meet survivors at desert rendezvous afterwards.

The LRDG owed nothing to anyone. Its founders were pre-war explorers, some civilian, who liked the desert. They had learned hard lessons about navigating through it, driving over it and surviving in it. Formally raised in September 1940, the LRDG specialized in deep reconnaissance behind enemy lines, treading softly, hiding in the scrub, counting enemy tanks and trucks, noting index numbers, men carried, regimental symbols and much else. This information was relayed to GHQ by radio. When necessary, the LRDG would shoot its way out of trouble. When appropriate, it would raid enemy airfields or convoys. It was led by intelligent men who did not mind sharing their knowledge with other special forces, including the piratical Peniakov, founder of 'Popski's Private Army'. Popski later created chaos in Italy as well as the desert.

The partnership with the offensively-inclined SAS was fruitful. Operating from the LRDG base at the remote Jalo Oasis in the Libyan desert, Stirling's men struck at a series of airfields held by the Italians. One group, led by an Irish Rugby international, Paddy Mayne, blew up 24 aircraft and a petrol dump and then gatecrashed an officers' mess party into which they fired long bursts from Thompson sub-machine-guns. With no bombs left but frustrated by the sight of one aircraft still intact, Mayne, an abnormally strong man, ripped out the instrument panel 'as a souvenir', he later explained. Elsewhere, one officer and three men penetrated dense barbed wire to destroy 37 aircraft. From now on, the raiders were in business. By Christmas they were credited with the destruction of 90 aircraft and much other war material. Before the North African campaign ended, that total would rise to 400.

In January 1942, the SAS returned to its training base at Kabrit alongside the Suez Canal, where Stirling, now a major, was authorized to recruit 50 Free French paratroopers to enlarge his force. He also obtained personal approval for an SAS badge — the Sword of Damocles — and distinctive para wings. The same month he persuaded an amphibious reconnaissance force from 'Layforce', known then as the Special Boat Section, to lend him a captain and a corporal to attack shipping in Buerat harbour. The team's collapsible canoe collapsed prematurely during a long, gruelling desert drive. Nevertheless, the two men laid bombs on 23 diesel lorries, eight small fuel dumps, a radio mast and station. Elsewhere in the port, the raiders destroyed many other petrol carriers.

By now, Stirling was gaining a reputation as a desert pimpernel. One of his officers, Fitzroy Maclean, wrote: 'No sooner was one operation completed than he was off on another. No sooner had the enemy become aware of his presence in one part of the desert and set about taking counter-measures, than he was attacking them somewhere else, always where they least expected it . . .' It was about this time that Stirling acquired a fleet of jeeps and fitted them with twin .303 Vickers machine-guns scrounged from RAF biplanes. The guns could fire 1,200 rounds a minute, and a long burst would cut a car in two. For a raid on Sidi-Enich airfield, Stirling drilled a team to drive eighteen jeeps at speed, only five yards apart, all 68 guns firing among Luftwaffe aircraft parked neatly beside the runways. The effect was similar to that of Drake's broadsides on the

Spanish Armada: the targets were torn to pieces by the weight of firepower.

Stirling was also cunning in the ways of military politics and remarkably persuasive. Not only did he achieve a working partnership with the LRDG, but in due course he would also lure the SBS into his organization as well as a Greek special force, the 'Sacred Squadron', composed of soldiers who had escaped from their country after the Nazi invasion. There was also, briefly, a Special Interrogation Unit, comprising anti-Nazi Germans who wore the uniform and carried the equipment of Rommel's Afrika Korps. Unfortunately, on its first operation the SIG was betrayed along with other SAS men by a traitor within its own ranks. The experiment was not repeated.

The overall success of the SAS brought with it the problem that GHQ in Cairo wanted to lock its operations into the preparations for El Alamein, the battle that was to turn the tide of German success in North Africa. Stirling's men cut the coastal railway behind German lines on thirteen out of the twenty days preceding the battle, but a much more ambitious scheme promoted by headquarters demonstrated that it did not yet comprehend what Stirling was about. The scheme started to push the SAS back towards the idea of big, set-piece commando raids with everything but a military band in attendance. The unit was tasked to participate, in the autumn of 1942, in a combined operation involving two Royal Navy destroyers, commandos, SBS, LRDG, the Sudan Defence Force and the RAF. The SAS would attack Benghazi and Tobruk from the desert, while the SBS and commandos came in from the sea. As an LRDG officer later wrote, such a large operation could not be kept secret: 'I was horrified how unwieldy the thing had become.' There is good reason to believe that the security of the operation was 'blown' well in advance. Stirling's column was ambushed and trapped on a mined road before it reached its target and had to fight its way out. At Tobruk, most of those who landed were taken prisoner. Three SBS survivors marched 400 miles across the desert to elude capture. Most of that distance they covered in bare feet. The march lasted 78 agonising days.

A few weeks later, Jack Sillitoe, an SAS soldier with one of Mayne's raiding parties, was cut off by the enemy while laying demolition charges on a railway near Tobruk. He, too, decided to march back across the desert rather than surrender. For eight days he walked, drinking his own urine to avoid dying of thirst, and lapping up dew that had collected on discarded petrol drums. At last, after 180 miles, he reached an LRDG supply dump hidden in a wadi. 'Just as I got there', he said later, 'it began to rain. Oh, what a joy! What a relief . . .' He was found by the SAS and recovered within two weeks.

By January 1943, the SAS was a formally recognized regiment and about to emerge as a brigade with the creation of 2 SAS, commanded by David's brother, William. Such are the misfortunes of war that, in February 1943, David Stirling was discovered in a cave in Tunisia by an anti-SAS patrol on exercise. Stirling had been moving at night and

6-17. Kabrit, an obscure village near the Suez Canal, was where it all began in 1941. Many recruits to the SAS were already qualified army commandos. This cut no ice with Colour Sergeant Glaze, an Army Physical Training Instructor who ran the Regiment's first battle course. There was the low wire to be negotiated (**6**); a scaffold catwalk (**7**) with a long drop at the end of it; the rope bridge (**8**); the trench below more wire, passing through a terrifyingly realistic 'minefield' (**9**); followed by a sprint to the log bridge (**10, 11**); then a leopard crawl to the monkey walk (**12, 13**); the second trench (**14**); the wall (**15, 16**) and, finally, the firing point (**17**), where marksmanship was tested while lungs, arms and nerves were still shattered.

△6

△9

△10

△14

△15

sleeping concealed by day. He was woken by a nervous man whose shaking hand held a pistol close to his head. Four subsequent escape attempts by Stirling finally led to his imprisonment in Colditz. His deputy, Mayne, took over command of 1 SAS and fought with it for the rest of the war. The number to survive so long could be counted on the fingers of one badly mutilated hand.

Stirling's capture was a disaster for the SAS. He, alone, could hold together the diverse, dynamic people he had recruited. John Lodwick, an SBS officer, wrote later: 'With the capture of Stirling chaos ensued. That is not too strong a word for it. A great and powerful organization had been built up but it had been an organization controlled and directed by a single man. Stirling alone knew where everybody was, what they were doing and what he subsequently intended them to do. When he disappeared, his adjutant, Captain Bill Blyth, Scots Guards, spent nearly two months clearing up outstanding business. A consignment of jeeps would arrive: Stirling had ordered them and had obviously earmarked them for somebody, but nobody now knew for whom. The squabbles over the previous transport would become bitter, to be interrupted for a moment by a party reporting from Sousse or Tabarca or the Fezzan and demanding further instructions. No one except David

△7

△8

△11

△12

△13

△16

△17

Stirling and their commander was absolutely sure what they had been doing there in the first place. These were not the results of inefficiency, but of control by a powerful personality with a hundred different irons in a very cramped fire. Stirling, alone, had known the whole story. His capture was catastrophic.'

Other SAS veterans of that period believe that Lodwick's description is an exaggeration. However it is certain that as a result of Stirling's capture, the SAS now underwent one of its characteristic evolutions to meet changed circumstances. The SBS regained its independence, becoming the Special Boat Squadron. It retained the SAS beige beret,

badge and wings, as did the Greek 'Sacred Squadron' which joined forces with it. Mayne's men became, for a time, the Special Raiding Squadron. William Stirling's 2 SAS Regiment was formally created in Algeria in April 1943, a couple of months after David's capture. The SBS would take the islands of the Aegean and the Adriatic as its operational zone from now on, working from time to time with the LRDG. The men serving under Mayne and Bill Stirling would fight in Sicily, Italy (where the two units finally met) and in North-West Europe after D-Day.

△18

18. SAS soldiers had to be as familiar with enemy weapons as their own — a tradition which continues today — because they would operate behind enemy lines without resupply for long periods. Here, they demonstrate for visiting top brass their ability to strip down and reassemble a variety of such weapons. Stirling (standing third from left) briefs the visitors. The soldiers, recruited from various units, wear a variety of headgear, including forage caps and tam-o'-shanter.

19,20. Stirling believed in parachuting as the quickest, surest method of placing his teams deep behind enemy lines. He would be proved right eventually, but his first and only desert parachute operation, in foul weather, was a disaster. Before he could test his theory, he had to train his parachutists. With no special facilities available at Kabrit in the early days, he and his colleagues indulged in some characteristically lateral thinking. Parachute exit drills were practised from stationary aircraft (**19**); landing falls from the back of a fast-moving lorry (**20**).

21-24. Parachuting as such was a more hazardous business for the SAS pioneers than it is for today's military jumpers who have a variety of techniques to assist them. Each man made his descent with no second, emergency reserve parachute mounted on his chest. He carried a single parachute in a container on his back, and if that failed to deploy, he died. The exit was usually a small,

round hole in the floor of an RAF bomber. The soldier who misjudged his exit sometimes smashed his nose as he went out and occasionally lost his front teeth as well. The experience was known jokingly as 'ringing the bell'. Later, the men would carry heavy equipment attached to their bodies. If they were not able to release this on its rope before they landed, they were grievously injured. In France, later in the war, many casualties resulted from this. Here, SAS men stand by to parachute from a Wellington (November 1942). The red light is on (**21**) and the soldier knows he has just five seconds left before . . . 'Green light on. Go!' He plunges feet first down the hole. Behind him a static line attached to the aircraft pays out and then rips his parachute container open (**22**). Hundreds of feet below, the desert drop zone's 'T' marker can be seen to the right of the parachutist. Now, safely down (**23**), he collapses his canopy. In erratic desert wind conditions some men were dragged along the ground after a safe landing and injured after they thought they were safe. Weak with relief that his first jump is over, the SAS parachutist gets out of his harness to 'field pack' the gear (**24**). In action, he would simply hit the quick-release box to free himself, snatch up his weapon and go straight into action, if necessary. Behind enemy lines, if he had not been seen, he would bury the parachute.

△19 △20

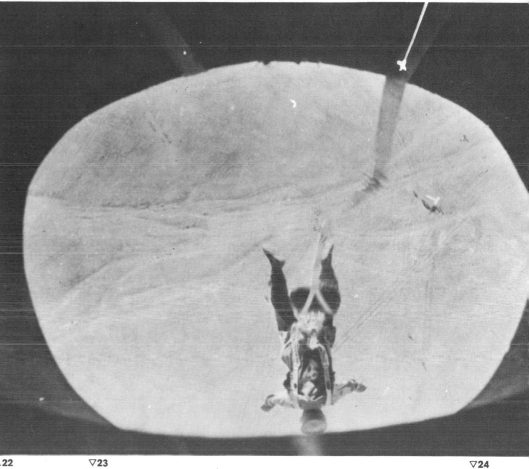

△21 △22 ▽23 ▽24

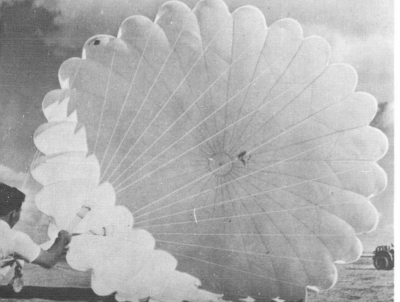

25. The survivors of the first, unsuccessful parachute raid — an attempt to attack Rommel's Libyan air bases at Gazala and Tmimi — included Stirling himself. The men were picked up in the desert by the Long Range Desert Group, which subsequently carried the SAS to many of its target areas. The LRDG, although it also put in some highly successful raids on its own account, was primarily a group of reconnaissance specialists, particularly skilled in enduring exhausting road watches on Afrika Korps traffic. Some LRDG soldiers joined the SAS. This photograph was taken on 25 May 1942.

26-29. In the summer of 1942, the SAS acquired its own transport, a fleet of light, agile, American-made jeeps. These had the great advantage in desert conditions of four-wheel drive. They were less likely to become bogged down at times when a raiding party was being pursued on the ground or attacked from the air, or both. SAS jeeps carried at the rear twin .303 Vickers K machine-guns taken from old RAF aircraft, and a .5 Browning machine-gun at the front. Jerrycans holding 90 gallons of petrol, exposed to the incendiary effect of enemy tracer bullets, as well as 60lb of high-explosive for demolition, were just two more routine risks that SAS desert veterans lived with. Men such as Corporal James McDiarmid on the Vickers gun (**26**) and his fellow Scot, Corporal John Henderson (formerly Scots Guards) manning the Browning (**27**) were natural optimists. The contrast between a typical LRDG Ford truck (**28**) and an SAS jeep (**29**) is vividly drawn by these photographs.

30. To hit their targets, SAS patrols, such as this one from the Greek 'Sacred Squadron', drove for hundreds of miles across the desert, whose maps contained many blank areas. Navigation by sun compass or the stars had to be exact. Water was conserved by attaching a condenser to the jeep's radiator, a trick learned from the LRDG. The hot water drained into the condenser — a drum fitted to the front grille — where it cooled before going back into the system. Rations for 60 days were carried.

31. Attacking under cover of darkness, the raiders reduced airfields and railways to a mass of tangled wreckage. Enemy aircraft such as those discovered by the advancing Eighth Army near Sidi Barrani in November 1942, after the Battle of El Alamein, was customary evidence of an SAS visit. According to the author Philip Warner, the principal railway between Tobruk and Mareth was blown up so many times that GHQ in Cairo, mindful of the railway's value to the advancing Eighth Army, told Stirling's men to leave it alone. 'It was rare to get a reply from the SAS but this time it came very quickly. "Very sorry. Railway blown up at X, Y, and Z. Couldn't resist it!"'

△**25**

△**26** ▽**27**

▽28　　　　　　　　　　　　　　　　　　　　　　　　　　　　　　　　　　　　▽29　△30

▽31

△32 ▽33

△34 ▽35

▽36

32. The SAS had other even more exotic allies. These included Lieutenant-Colonel John Haselden (disguised in Arab dress, with LRDG vehicle in the background). Haselden, officially an adviser on Arab affairs to the Eighth Army, ran a network of agents in towns and villages occupied by the enemy. He also commanded a mixed force, including SBS men at Tobruk during the ill-fated raid on that city and Benghazi (see p. 9). Haselden died leading a charge against an enemy strongpoint. Tommy Langton and two other SBS men, Privates Watler and Hillman, who had been in the same action with Haselden, marched for 78 days across the desert to elude capture.

33. During the six extraordinary months after El Alamein in October 1942, Montgomery's Eighth Army advanced 1,000 miles to Tunisia to link up with Alexander's First Army and finally win North Africa. Rommel's last major defensive position against the Eighth Army was the French-built Mareth Line, 170 miles west of Tripoli. In January 1943, the LRDG found a key route round this fortification, across firm desert to the south. The first British troops to arrive in the area, as this 1942 photograph implies, were these men of 'B' Squadron, 1 SAS, seen here at one of the line's strongpoints. Their commander is on the right, wearing a white coat. The joker with the revolver (left) is not identified.

34, 35. The cost of such operations, in terms of the hardship suffered by some SAS soldiers, was terrifying. When all went well and they returned successfully, they could afford to smile, like the two cleaning their weapons (**34**), but things did not always go according to plan. Corporal Jack Sillito was with a party attempting to blow up a railway. Sillito and his lieutenant crept up to those guarding the railway, to kill them as a preliminary to the demolition job. The lieutenant's tommy-gun jammed and he was killed as both men came under fire. With no food or water, Sillito began the long march back to sanctuary, well over 100 miles. According to a contemporary account, 'It started to rain and he was soaked to the skin. Starting to walk at 2pm, he had covered 25 miles by dawn next day. He tried to sleep but could not, so he walked all that day, covering another 30 miles. During the next night he covered a further 20 miles, still without food or water. A puddle saved him for a time but a tin of bully beef which he found in an abandoned truck was useless to him as he could not swallow.' (Later, Sillito said he had kept the tin. 'It came in handy for holding my urine, which I then started to drink.') The contemporary account says that 'the remaining distance . . . was a horrible nightmare, of falling unconscious many times, lying helpless for long periods, too weak to stand, giving up once and preparing to die, being saved by rain, and much more that is not clear due to (his) delerium . . .' Eight days after the beginning of the nightmare, Sillito was found unconscious, but just alive, by SAS comrades in a wadi used by them and the LRDG as a rendezvous and secret emergency store.

This picture of Sillito (**35**) was taken some days after he had been discharged from hospital, November 1942.

36. Survival in the desert behind enemy lines often depended upon the existence of secret rendezvous and mini bases of the sort at which Sillito was found. This one, not far from a German headquarters at Benghazi, was in a cave beneath a desert rock formation. Sunlight shining through a circular hole in the rock made it particularly convenient. This photograph of SAS soldiers with rucksacks and sleeping bags (right, foreground) was taken at Easter 1942, several months before the successful British counter-attack at El Alamein.

37. When the forward elements of the two Allied armies finally linked up in the Gabes-Tozeur area of Tunisia, it was Corporal Race, an SAS radio operator (left) who represented the Eighth Army. He is seen here with a French sergeant-major from Tozeur.

38. One man was not present to celebrate the Allied victory when it came in May 1943. David Stirling, seen here in one of the most famous SAS war photographs, with a raiding party led by Lieutenant Edward McDonald (formerly Cameron Highlanders), took the same chances as his men. In Tunisia, the greatest risk was of betrayal by Arabs who were hostile, or bribed, or both. Stirling was captured in February, only a few weeks before Rommel's defeat and, after several escape attempts, incarcerated in Colditz for the rest of the war. This photograph, familiar though it may seem, was in fact the last one of Stirling before his capture, taken on 18 January 1943. The official contemporary caption reads: 'Lieutenant-Colonel David Stirling, OC of the SAS in the Middle East, greeting a patrol on its safe return'.

▽**37**

▽**38**

Aegean and Adriatic, 1943–1944
'Yarnder loom the islands'

The SBS — at various times it was the Special Boat Section, the Folboat Section, the Special Boat Service and, finally, the Special Boat Squadron of 1 SAS Regiment — included some of the most charismatic people involved in irregular warfare during a vintage period, when such warfare enjoyed more official backing than at any time before or since. Typical among them was J. N. ('Jock') Lapraik, a Doctor of Law, who was awarded an OBE in addition to his DSO and two MCs. Like many of his successors in the SAS, he privately construed the regimental motto to read, 'Who Trains Wins'. Some of the training he provided at a special warfare school in Malta immediately before he and many of his pupils joined the SBS in the spring of 1943 was so near the reality of warfare as to make very little difference. After the war, he commanded 21 SAS (TA). It was an astonishing career for someone who had been crippled in childhood by tuberculosis.

The first leader of the SBS after the capture of David Stirling and the regimental diaspora that followed it was Earl Jellicoe, son of the admiral. Some six months earlier, already on Stirling's team, George Jellicoe and others raided Heraklion airfield on Crete to destroy Luftwaffe bombers then preparing to attack a vital convoy sailing to Malta. Detected by German guards on the airport perimeter wire, Jellicoe lay flat and snored. The guards assumed he was a Cretan drunk and went on their way. With a team of French SAS men, Jellicoe then insinuated his way into bomb-proof aircraft shelters and laid charges that destroyed sixteen aircraft. Later, all six raiders were betrayed and trapped. After climbing two mountain ranges and marching 120 miles, Jellicoe and a Greek guide were the only survivors.

Jellicoe led the SBS in a campaign scarred during its first phase by other people's strategic blunders, and one which was burnished with repeated success in its second phase. During the first phase — one of several months' duration from September 1943, when the Italian Government surrendered — the SBS successively occupied and then retreated from a series of islands in the Dodecanese group, off Turkey. Many of these were controlled by the Italians alone or in an increasingly uneasy partnership with their erstwhile German allies. A brief occupation of the largest of these islands, Rhodes, was followed by similar events in Kos, Leros, Samos, Calinos, Simi and Khalki. Along the way, the Italians usually double-crossed old and new allies impartially.

Rhodes was a thorn in the side of the British for most of the war. The original commando group, 'Layforce', had been first brought to the Middle East to try to capture the place. In 1943, after the Italian Government's surrender, Jellicoe was parachuted into Rhodes accompanied by just one signaller and one interpreter, who broke his leg on landing. The task was to persuade the Italian governor not to hand over control of Rhodes to a German garrison there. As they descended, at night, the three men were shot at by Italians, who missed. Jellicoe's efforts to persuade an Italian force of 35,000 men to resist 10,000 Germans failed because British

GHQ in Cairo, directing overall strategy, turned down his pleas for rapid Allied reinforcement to boost Italian morale. As one participant in the campaign wrote later, 'George Jellicoe . . . had sent many signals to Cairo asking for only a few troops to help him, but all his entreaties had fallen on unhearing ears . . . We made our first of many blunders in so impotently failing to assume control over Rhodes . . . This failure to get airfields on it should have been the signal that those Aegean operations were doomed to disaster unless Turkey could be persuaded at once to come in on the side of the Allies.'

The Turks were willing to turn a blind eye to the piratical SBS caiques and schooners lying up in coves along their shores, but they were also determined to remain formally neutral. So, without sufficient air cover, the islands that the SBS had liberated were bombed into submission and defeat again by an unopposed Luftwaffe operating from neighbouring Rhodes. In spite of this, the first phase of the SBS campaign had one great advantage for Allied strategy. Instead of resting comfortably in their beds, the Germans had to be constantly on the watch for the next surprise attack, usually by night. Their garrisons had to be reinforced. By the end of 1943, six divisions of Wehrmacht soldiers — around 60,000 men desperately needed to defend Nazi-held Italian and Balkan territory — were tied up in the Dodecanese. As one SBS man put it later, 'The Germans were wearing their boots out on sentry duty.' In this sense at least, the first wave of SBS attacks was a classic of guerrilla warfare and there was nothing the might of air power could do to stop them.

On 20 January 1944, the SBS schooner *Tewfik*, a slow and ugly vessel, left Beirut carrying 4,700lb of explosive for the next series of raids. She was accompanied by a variety of launches. The first of these attacks, which were to imprison the German garrisons on the islands by destroying their shipping, was led by a legendary Dane named Anders Lassen. Where Lassen went, so did Sean O'Reilly of the Irish Guards. (Many wartime SAS men were citizens of the Irish Republic who had volunteered to fight for Britain.) Lassen and O'Reilly made an odd but devastatingly successful fighting partnership: Lassen, the high-born and unruly product of a stately home who was lethal with bow and arrow by the age of twelve; Guardsman O'Reilly, a hard, professional soldier now aged 42 and twenty years older than the officer to whom he was devoted. Lassen, the hunter, hated Germans and was already hardened by raids on the Channel Islands and Vichy French Africa as well as the Middle East. O'Reilly just liked a good fight.

On 31 January, with two other men and an interpreter, they landed on Khalki, broke into the police station, took prisoner those within as well as seizing their weapons and anything else of military value. Lassen was disappointed that the action was so tame. Then a German launch entered harbour. The SBS team shot it up, wounding two of the six men on board. With their prisoners and booty they then returned to Turkey aboard this vessel, Lassen having been wounded in the foot by a shot from O'Reilly.

39, 40. Scenes at Lapraik's special warfare school, fort of Manuel de Vilhena, Malta, 21 April 1943, which some people found tougher than actual operations. Armed with characteristic commando weapons, including Thompson submachine-guns and fighting knives, the men had to undergo a battle course that included jumping over blazing oil drums piled several feet high (**39**), or use rope suspended high above the harbour while being 'bombed' (**40**). Live ammunition was often used in such training. Some veterans were allowed to carry their own, highly personal weapons.

At another island, Stampalia, an SBS team wormed its way through a minefield before swimming out to German shipping, which it blew up. On Simi, Lieutenant David Clark and Sergeant Miller killed ten card-playing Germans with grenades. These men had responded to Clark's civil invitation to them to surrender by shooting at him. On Lipsoi and nearby Arkoi, Captain Bruce Mitford and five men blew up two merchant ships carrying German supplies. The third, loaded with champagne and beer destined for Wehrmacht officers, they seized. On Piscopi, nine Germans were shot as they fled from one SBS team into an ambush laid by another. On Nisiros, Major Ian Patterson intervened when the Germans arrived to clear an orphanage of its children and remove them to Rhodes. The children were taken into the hills. The SBS moved into the orphanage and waited. Outside, the children's luggage was piled as if for the journey. Five Germans were killed and seventeen taken prisoner in the subsequent battle in and around the building.

In April, the SBS turned its attention to the Cyclades group of islands in the southern Aegean. Under the command of David Sutherland, simultaneous raids were made by night on radio stations on the islands of Mikonos, Santorini, Ios and Amorgos. Anders Lassen and Sergeant Nicholson hit a billet containing 48 Italians and 20 Germans on the first floor of the Bank of Athens in Santorini. As the

SBS veteran John Lodwick tells the story, 'First Nicholson would kick the door open . . . then Lassen would throw two grenades inside . . . then Nicholson, firing his Bren (machinegun) from the hip, would spray the walls and corners . . . Finally, Lassen, with his pistol, would deal with any remaining signs of life.' Of the twelve men in the SBS back-up party for this massacre, one officer and one sergeant were killed and two wounded. Overall, the operation caused 41 enemy fatalities, 27 wounded and 19 prisoners. The SBS lost two killed and three wounded out of a raiding force of 39 men. There were similar scenes soon afterward on Paros, where Lassen was leading, and on Naxos.

When the Germans increased the island garrisons, the SBS response, in July, was an ambitious raid on Simi by 81 British soldiers and 139 of the Greek 'Sacred Squadron'. Part of this force induced the occupants of a castle to surrender. When the SBS withdrew, they took 151 prisoners with them and left 21 enemy dead. Six SBS men were wounded. Later the same month, Crete became the target. Landings were made at five points on the coast and some

days later, on 23 July, seven petrol dumps containing 165,000 gallons of fuel were destroyed. In all, 32 German defenders were killed and three wounded. The raid was one in which the element of surprise was pared down to a minimum. The SBS men had barely penetrated to the target areas when they were detected. Confused gun battles followed in and around the dumps, while two men from each team methodically placed time bombs where they would do most damage.

The raid was also notable for some savage hand-to-hand fighting. Lodwick, who was taken prisoner on this occasion, recounts: 'A man with a fixed bayonet was attempting to hold up Private Stewart. Stewart reported, "I grabbed his rifle with my left hand and shot him five times in the stomach with my carbine. Jock Asbery hit two of the other sentries. The rest scuttled . . ." Asbery made good his escape but as Stewart was crawling away through the wire, a sentry leapt on top of him, shouting. "We struggled for some time", said Stewart. "After a while I managed to draw my knife. I put it in his stomach and he fell, but still

▽**41**

shouting".' Lodwick was kept in solitary confinement after this raid and subjected to a mock execution in an effort to loosen his tongue. He finally escaped from a prison camp in Serbia, destroying a railway bridge on his way back. 'After 134 days we returned to the unit', Lodwick recounts. "Ah, you're back", said Jellicoe. "Damned slow about it, weren't you?"'

In August 1944, the SBS moved its base to Italy and began raids into occupied Yugoslavia, but the unit was far from finished with the Aegean area. One squadron, under Lassen, cleared the sea approaches and islands off mainland Greece. Another, under Ian Patterson, parachuted into Araxos airfield near Patras. Next day, Jellicoe landed there more conventionally. A race was now on to liberate Athens, and then the rest of Greece. According to one version, Jellicoe and Patterson were the first Allied soldiers to enter the Greek capital, on pedal cycles; another suggests that it was Lassen.

As a mixed force of SBS men, paras and RAF Regiment soldiers pressed on they had to fight a mobile but increas-ingly orthodox war against the German rearguard. Lassen remained unorthodox. To enter Salonika, north of Athens, as fast as possible (he had come by way of the Sporades Islands) he seized four fire-engines. When he caught up with the rearguard, he killed eight Germans. His second in command, Lieutenant J. C. Henshaw, killed eleven.

The mixed force, commanded by Jellicoe, now divided into two columns, one fighting under Lieutenant-Colonel Coxon, the other under Patterson making a frontal assault, Foreign Legion style, on a hill position at Kozani. The two groups linked up again above a mountain pass on the border with Yugoslavia. 'The German column, on foot and in horse-drawn vehicles, was moving through a narrow defile', Lodwick writes. SBS jeeps, armed with Browning machine-guns, were drawn up on the covering slopes. 'It took a long time, later, to count the German dead.'

From this series of pictures of the SBS in action on different Aegean islands, it is possible to reconstruct a typical operation, step by step, and the preparations for it.

41. The base for most SAS operations was the Levant schooner *Tewfik*, or a Greek caique, often moored quietly in neutral, Turkish waters. The men were allowed ashore, but they had to stay close to their base. This 'shore leave', such as it was, gave them the chance to dry freshly washed clothes on bushes (foreground). The SBS veteran, John Lodwick, describes other typical activities on board, on a quiet day: '. . . Lassen, naked, making a bow for use in pig-hunting; in a cabin below, David Sutherland — Jellicoe's second-in-command and successor as commanding officer — pipe in mouth, writing an opera-tional order; a typewriter clacking nearby; O'Reilly and friends on deck, discussing "good old days" in Libya, German prisoners in the forepeak, waiting for a cigarette; an SBS officer zeroing a German sniper rifle.'

42. When an operation was in the wind, a fast, rakish Royal Navy launch would often lie alongside the schooner. This would ferry a raiding party to within a few hundred yards of the target island, after which the SBS party would go ashore in canoes or inflatables. This photograph was taken along the Turkish coast opposite Simi.

43. Not all SBS or SAS operations were planned in detail, but many were. The large ones brought together the big names, such as Jellicoe (centre) and Tsigantes (left), commanding the Greek 'Sacred Squadron'.

△42 ▽43

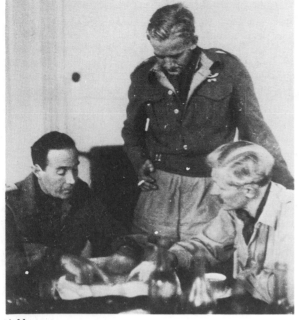

△44

△45

△46

△49

△50

44. The discussions continued after dinner. Anders Lassen (standing) with Colonel Max Bally (left) and another SBS officer, plan the withdrawal from Samos.

45. Not all the raiders were British. Many were Greeks of the 'Sacred Squadron', who were selected and trained as SAS men and wore the same cap badge. Their commander was Colonel Kristodoulus Tsigantes, DSO, of the Greek Army, seen here in the Aegean on 28 July 1944.

46. The kit is put together as they smoke and gossip. Parachutists S. W. Shepherd (right) and Weddell prime hand grenades with detonators aboard *Tewfik*, in preparation for a raid on Famiana, 28 July 1944.

47. The target, as usual, is an island: Simi. They have been there before. It is manned by a mixed Italian and German garrison. The

chances are that the Italians will surrender; the Germans will fight.

48. The town is dominated by a 20mm machine-gun (ringed on the left), manned by Germans. On the mountain, right, another enemy strongpoint is marked on this wartime air reconnaissance photograph, taken on 13 September 1943.

49. The raiding party departs. Lassen, smoking when he is not fighting or hunting, stands in the stern, sniffing action.

50. It is almost time to go into action. The sappers, with enough explosive in their rucksacks to blow up the Simi machine-gun and much else, prepare to disembark.

51. The rest of the party follows. This image is from Famiana, 28 July 1944; the process does not vary much from one island to another, even if some people prefer sandals to Army boots.

△47 ▽48

◁51

△52

△55 △56

52. Ashore, undetected . . . The first assault, on an enemy billet, is about to go in. Those who will smash through the front door are covered every inch of the way by their comrades on a slope overlooking the target. Any enemy survivors who try to flee will be picked off as they emerge. Simi, 1943.

53. The SBS men at the sharp end have other allies. Most Greek partisans are characters; some, like this Samos guerrilla, instinctively produce a bravura performance for the camera.

54. The attack on Simi goes in and the casualties mount. Some, like these Italians, show that they, too, have courage as they remove their wounded under fire. Their weapons are abandoned and the Red Cross flag — of which several are instantly available — is substituted.

55. Some carabineri are happy to give themselves up as prisoners before they are wounded. This group is even more happy to accept cigarettes from one of their captors, an SBS sapper. Simi, 1943.

56. As the fighting continues, there are

more casualties to be removed. While an SBS team extracts tactical information from the locals (background), the Italians disconsolately take a wounded comrade away for treatment. But this time they are not under fire. They carry the injured man on a bench used as a makeshift stretcher. Simi, 1943.

57. Not everyone surrenders immediately or gladly. When the SBS hit Naxos on 1 November 1944, they seized a Wehrmacht sergeant-major. His men could not believe they should surrender. To check the

△53

△54

57▷

truth of the order they sent two of their number, still armed, as a truce party to find out. The German soldiers rowed out to discuss the matter with the SBS and their captive sergeant-major. Then, reluctantly, they also became prisoners of war.

△58 ▽59 △60

58. Before the Germans on Simi are marched away, they bury their dead and, near to tears, honour the casualties with a Nazi salute.

59. For the SBS victors, relief that the raid is over . . . But although the danger has passed for the time being, the .30mm M1 carbine and unbuckled British service revolver remain instantly ready. In irregular warfare, you just never know when someone will open fire . . .

60. Up on the hill, meanwhile, an SBS sapper sergeant checks on the condition of that 20mm gun, after he has blown it up. If the Germans return, they will not find the piece in working order.

61. The 'wash up' ritual after each operation varied from job to job, island to island. On Khios, the streets were mined. The SBS defused them (1 November 1944).

62. After the shooting, an SBS head-quarters is set up in a cave, a necessary precaution against the near certainty of German air attack. From the cave, food is distributed to civilians. One soldier, a hearts-and-mind specialist, makes friends with a local baby. His comrade gives the child its first sweet. Mother tries not to look apprehensive.

△61

△62

△63

63. Not all SBS raids had such a happy ending. During the first phase of the unit's island-storming campaign in 1943, the seizure of an island invariably led to bombing raids by Luftwaffe Stukas only a few minutes flying time away from their base on Rhodes. Such intensive bombing was often followed by German reoccupation and vicious reprisals. It was during such an air attack on Samos that Anders Lassen (standing) and his men sheltered in a drainage ditch. Lassen was relaxed while under fire, tense when trapped in headquarters with no action in sight.

Here, to pass the time, he expounds his next bright idea for killing Nazis. Some of his men wonder if they heard him correctly. In this, as in many other photographs, the wartime censor has erased the SAS cap badge and other insignia — such as the flag fluttering from *Tewfik* on p. 20 to obscure the identity of the unit involved.

Italy and North-West Europe, 1943-1944
Partisans v. Panzers

After the D-Day landings in France on 6 June 1944, the battle for North-West Europe became the focus of popular, and later, historical attention. For this reason, the battle for Italy, Greece, Yugoslavia and Albania was an almost forgotten chapter of the Second World War. Yet that campaign, in particular the last, bitterly cold winter campaign of 1944–45, was one in which the SAS was involved until the end of the war, and one in which the future of those countries would be shaped as much by political activity before liberation as by the military process of liberation itself. The impact of individual SAS soldiers made a profound impression upon even those partisans not in sympathy with the British Government and, in the case of Yugoslavia, contributed to a rejection of post-war Soviet imperialism. It was the first of many such campaigns that the SAS would wage. It was also a period of tactical mistakes and hard lessons, as well as useful technical innovation in the art of irregular warfare behind enemy lines. Finally, it was the only campaign in which the three British arms of the regiment — 1 SAS, 2 SAS and the SBS — all participated.

From the end of the war in North Africa until the Allied invasion of Sicily in July 1943, 1 SAS, under Mayne, retrained in Palestine and the Gulf of Aqaba, practising rock climbing and amphibious warfare. Bill Stirling's 2 SAS, meanwhile, cut its teeth on amphibious raids — not all successful — on the still-occupied islands of Sardinia, Sicily, Lampedusa and Pantelleria. They were transported by submarines, fast torpedo-boats and slow, terribly fragile canoes. Soon afterwards, during the main Allied landings on Sicily, SAS groups of fewer than ten men dropped by parachute and paralysed communications in the enemy rear, blowing up railway lines, attacking convoys, mining roads and shooting-up convoys. But here, as in Italy a few months later, lack of two-way radio, or a system of marking resupply drop zones, as well as aircrew error, made reliable resupply all but impossible. Without ammunition, these raiding parties had to make their way back to friendly territory as best they could. For many, it was a one-way mission.

Amphibious groups of SAS men, used as the cutting edge of the main invasion force, fared better, though this role as 'shock troops' raised yet again the controversy over the real function of the Regiment. At Marro di Porco, men of 1 SAS, outnumbered fifty to one, killed 100 enemy, took 600 prisoners and captured three coastal batteries. The Regiment's casualties were one killed and six wounded. In September 1943, after the Italian Government's surrender, the SAS began to raid targets behind enemy lines, sometimes fighting with partisans, but more often alone. As long as the front remained fluid, the SAS would grope for a route that permitted it to penetrate by jeep. When this was impossible, they landed by parachute or small boats, including fishing craft. Casualties on such operations were high; of those taken prisoner, many were subsequently executed.

Typical of penetration operations through the front line, rather than over or round it, was a fighting reconnaissance by men of 2 SAS under Roy Farran during the Allied advance from Taranto. Looking for a hole in the German line, Farran discovered an unguarded railway tunnel beneath an enemy hill position. He went in alone but turned back half way, alarmed by the sound of a machine-gun battle at his rear. Next day, Captain Jim Mackie and eleven men went forward along the same route, leaving two men to cover the exit. They found themselves, on the far side of the tunnel, in the middle of a German battalion. Mackie 'had time to inspect their defences at close range before he bumped a sentry. Both Jim and the German forgot to extract the pins from the grenades they threw. . . . The patrol fought its way back to the tunnel to find its mouth occupied by a German section. The two men left on guard had fled back to safety. . . . Mackie's party fought its way back to our side of the mountain . . . with grenades bursting in the cutting and tracer bullets whinging into the darkness of the tunnel.' The senior of the two lookouts, Farran's Cockney batman, was immediately expelled from the SAS and returned to his original unit, 'a broken man'.

For its next trick, as the line stabilized, 2 SAS ran a series of seaborne operations along the Adriatic coast between Ancona and Termoli to rescue many Allied prisoners of war who had escaped, and blow up targets such as an important railway bridge near Rimini.

In October, 1 SAS combined with No. 3 Army Commando and 40 Royal Marine Commando in the seizure, behind German lines, of the important road/railway junction and town of Termoli. A bitter battle followed, for this 'coup de main' threatened German positions north of Rome. The Wehrmacht moved its 16th Panzer Division from reserve in Naples to retake Termoli 'at all costs and drive the British into the sea'. They failed, although this typical, set-piece infantry battle was not what the SAS was in business for. The action cost the SAS 21 dead, 24 wounded and 23 taken prisoner out of 207 men who had landed, for this time, the opposition was not a soft-centred Italian force but German paras. Farran, at the scene with 20 of his men from 2 SAS, was astonished by the ferocity of the counterattack. With his 20 men, plus six Bren machine-guns and a two-inch mortar, he resisted for three days a force of several hundred at short range, along a thousand-yard front. Farran's men had been in their position for a day, unable to dig foxholes, 'before we discovered that the railway engine and truck in the middle of our front was loaded with high explosive, ready to be detonated. I was terrified during the entire battle that it would be hit by a mortar bomb.'

Elsewhere, Paddy Mayne's men of 1 SAS were fighting an equally tough battle to hold a cross-roads, as well as the town itself. A veteran with a remarkable record of service with the Regiment, was with a section that was trapped in a dried-up river bed at dawn. He recalls the last order given to the section, before it split up, was 'Every man for himself!' While trying to escape, he came under fire on a road and dived back into the wadi. He landed in bushes and heard German lorries halt just above him, then orders shouted in German. After an hour, still hiding, he was hit by fragments

of bombs exploding nearby. Concluding that he was the target of a grenade attack he reluctantly emerged to give himself up, but as he crawled on to the road, he saw only four deserted German lorries. One, containing ammunition, was exploding. He wrote at the time: 'Everything was plain sailing from now on. I made my way across country towards the sea and eventually reached Termoli, where I contacted Brigade HQ and asked them to get a message through to SRS (1 SAS) stating what had happened.' What had happened was that the rest of the section was dead or captured. Meanwhile, the commander, Mayne, was fighting a highly personal battle nearby in which, with characteristic ferocity, he killed a dozen of the enemy.

In March 1944, both 1 and 2 SAS went to Britain to prepare for the invasion of France. In December, Farran's squadron of 2 SAS returned from occupied France to hit German targets in Italy, behind the Gothic Line. Farran was ordered not to lead this operation in person, but he felt a keen personal responsibility for the deaths of comrades he had directed into action from a safe distance. So, on this occasion, he arranged to fall 'accidentally' from a transport aircraft while ostensibly dispatching his parachutists over hostile territory. (The men on his conscience included Ross Littlejohn and his troop, parachuted into the Alps, caught by a ski patrol and shot in captivity. Others, more fortunate, had fought a winter campaign under Major R. Walker-Brown on the frozen Lombardy Plain north of Spezia. When his 33 men returned to Allied territory in February 1945, 6,000 troops were dedicated to their specific capture.)

In a valley north of Florence, Farran found a fragmented partisan army from which he created a battalion — 'a motley crowd of ruffians' — comprising 30 Russians, 40 Italians of various political allegiances, 24 British, one Norwegian and a Scottish piper. Stiffened by the SAS, the partisans learned to stand their ground when attacked and finally to follow Farran's men in a devastating raid on a German corps HQ. In launching this attack, Farran, not for the first time, disobeyed orders from Allied headquarters. Emulating Walker-Brown a few miles north, he was also introducing light artillery into irregular warfare. A light 75mm pack howitzer was delivered by parachute and fired from mountain positions to create havoc among retreating Wehrmacht columns, which were convinced that they were cut off by the main Allied forces.

64, 65. In preparation for the invasion of Sicily and Italy, 1 SAS — now temporarily renamed the Special Raiding Squadron — trained for mountain warfare in Palestine during the early summer of 1943 (**64**). Paddy Mayne, a hard man who had been with the Regiment since its inception and led many of the most successful desert raids, now took command of 1 SAS. He is seen here (**65**) in Palestine at that time with the unit's Medical Officer, Captain Gunn (left). Mayne survived the war, although he spent most of it leading from the front as a commander behind enemy lines. He died in a motor accident near his home in Northern Ireland soon after the war.

While 1 and 2 SAS were in action in Italy, the SBS, now commanded by Colonel David Sutherland, were hitting one fortified Adriatic island after another, as well as operating against enemy shipping and deep in the territories of Yugoslavia and Albania. The legendary Lassen was still busy and still leading, it seemed, a charmed life. His luck finally ran out less than a month before the war ended. Lassen had become bored by small-scale actions, however risky, and wanted to see something of large-scale, orthodox warfare. He volunteered to lead the assault on a peculiarly difficult target. Just before midnight on 8 April 1945, Lassen and sixty men started paddling canoes across Lake Commachio. The lake is about twenty miles long and fifteen miles wide and, at that time of year, of an average depth of only two feet. There is virtually no cover. On the northern side stood the German-held town of Commachio. Lassen's diversionary attack on this town, in the enemy rear, was to open up the Eighth Army's spring offensive on the main positions. At daylight, they burrowed into the mud and bracken of a small island less than 400yds from the German front line. Another 24 hours found them on another island, in the centre of enemy positions where they came under shell fire. That night, the third of their mission, urged on by a signal from HQ, Lassen and a small party landed on the road into Commachio. The road was narrow, and crossed a dam. There was no cover when the German machine-guns opened up. Lassen led his unwounded men in a series of attacks on two enemy pill-boxes, hurling grenades into them at close quarters. The crew of the third machine-gun shouted that they surrendered, but as Lassen walked towards them, they shot him. As he fell, he hurled grenades at them. His last order before he died was that his men should withdraw, if they could, to safety. He was awarded a posthumous Victoria Cross.

When 1 and 2 SAS arrived in Britain in March 1944, not everyone was happy with the way the regiment was evolving. For one thing, the original 100 were now part of a brigade that also included the French 3rd and 4th Parachute Battalions and a Belgian SAS squadron. (The foreign element of 2 SAS also contained, as well as Frenchmen, Poles and even Germans collected from the French Foreign Legion, but these men operated as British troops in British uniform.) The chronic problem of radio communication was partly solved by attaching to the new SAS Brigade a squadron from the GHQ reconnaissance signal unit, 'Phantom'. With this addition, the total strength of the SAS, including a brigade headquarters, was 2,500. To some of the desert veterans, it was beginning to resemble an orthodox commando brigade.

Parallel with this development, the military top brass were preparing a D-Day assignment for the SAS which — like much that had happened in Italy and Sicily — was incompatible with David Stirling's original, starkly simple concept of deep penetration by small, very expert parties. The D-Day assignment was to prevent or impede enemy reinforcements from reaching the Normandy beachhead. Bill Stirling, commanding 2 SAS, pushed his defence of the original concept to the point of resignation. He was succeeded by Brian Franks, a veteran of No. 8 Commando, of 'Phantom' and Termoli.

Ultimately, the generals gave way to the opposition in the SAS and the Regiment's role was rewritten. It was to operate deep in occupied France, Belgium, Holland and Italy to provide a disciplined core for the Resistance and, independently, to strike at places of its own choosing as well as tipping off the RAF about suitable targets. So it was that

between D-Day and November 1944 (five months) more than 90 per cent of SAS troops were parachuted in 780 air sorties, of which 600 were successful. Material dropped included 9,820 containers, 75 jeeps and two six-pounder guns. The drop heights were uncomfortably low, down to 300ft at times, and six aircraft were lost.

A secret report on this period reveals that a total SAS force of 2,000 men suffered 330 casualties. Enemy losses were 7,753 killed or seriously wounded; taken prisoner, 4,764; cut off and forced to surrender to the US Army, 18,000. Additionally, 7,600 motor vehicles, 29 locomotives and 89 railway goods wagons were destroyed, and railway lines cut in 164 places. The problem of radio communication — on which resupply from the air depended — was partly overcome with the help of the BBC, which smuggled coded messages for the SAS into a variety of programmes. The men in the field, using sets powered by hand generators, could transmit as long as they could keep turning the handle.

The summer of 1944 gave the Regiment a good start in France, in spite of driving rain and difficult dropping conditions. Where possible, the advance party of each SAS force was met by local Maquis. When targets had to be hit at short notice, as in Brittany, the soldiers were dropped 'blind' into their target area and expected to reach Allied lines when the job was completed.

The first of more than 40 operations in France that summer was 'Houndsworth', during which a 5,000 square mile area around Dijon was occupied between 7 June and 6 September. A total of 150 SAS men took part and one entire troop of 17 men was lost with an aircraft on 18 June. Contemporary intelligence reports reveal that enemy casualties, including a German general blown up by a land mine, totalled 220 for one SAS officer killed and four soldiers seriously wounded in action. The seventeen SAS men who died on their way to war were not counted. The stark statistics do not convey the extraordinary nature of the operations concerned. During 'Houndsworth', 'A' Squadron of 1 SAS discovered Rommel's headquarters. By radio they requested sniper rifles. Their message added: 'Please do not send another party for this. Consider it to be my pigeon'. The reply from Allied HQ read: 'Rommel affair regrettably vetoed. Special party will be detailed.' But Rommel's death, according to subsequent accounts, was due to his enemies in Nazi Germany.

Not all of 'A' Squadron's schemes were vetoed. The squadron blew up main line railways, and military trains travelling on them, 22 times; rescued 16 Allied aircrew and a British woman agent sent into France by SOE; trapped a Gestapo spy posing as a Belgian and armed 3,000 French Maquisards. The unit's most elegant coup was to cut the Nevers-Dijon telephone line regularly, while arranging for a civilian telephone of its own to be installed in a forest hideout. The telephone was on the Chalaux exchange and regularly used by SAS patrols reporting from the scenes of their operations. In the same wood, the regimental padre conducted services and even ran confirmation classes.

But 'Houndsworth' was far from a romp. For days the men involved marched on half rations, in pouring rain; then waited all night at clandestine resupply drop zones for flights which were cancelled. A lack of jeeps hampered the entire expedition. All the more galling, therefore, for the soldiers to see at least seven such vehicles destroyed by parachute failures. One jeep, dropped in a wood, was recovered only after 40 trees had been felled.

Death or permanent and disabling injury were always near. The report of Sergeant C. McGuinn on the death of his

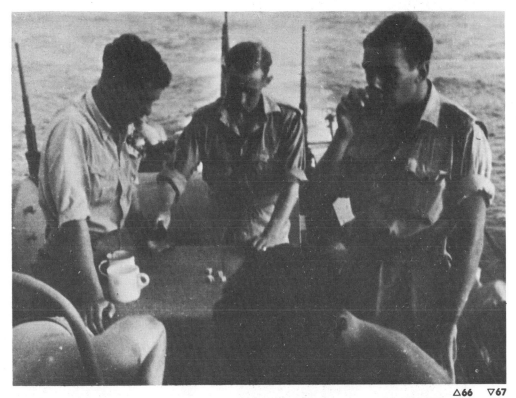

66, 67. On their way to assault Sicily from the sea in July 1943, a group of SAS officers relax with a game of poker dice (**66**): their target, a battery of coastal guns at Marro di Porco beneath which the entire invasion fleet would have to pass. It was vital that the guns be destroyed. A contemporary war diary records the tension before they went into action. 'We formed up on our mess decks. The Colonel bid us the best of luck and goodbye. The lights went out so as to get our eyes used to the darkness and so we sat, almost without a word . . . until over the loud-speaker came, "SRS, embark".' The SRS (1 SAS) were to have silenced just one gun battery. They destroyed two and captured a third intact, although they were out-numbered 50 to 1 by the Italian defenders. The first battery was set on fire by the first mortar round from the SAS. A total of 600 prisoners were taken. Simul-taneously, British prisoners from the glider force were liberated from communication tunnels beneath the guns. Before they left, the SAS were allowed a more relaxed look at their target, at close quarters (**67**).

△**66**　▽**67**

△68

△69

△70 ▽71

officer, Captain Bradford, illustrates this. With Bradford, Sergeant White, DCM, MM, and two Maquisards, McGuinn was driving a jeep loaded with primed explosive along a quiet country road near the village of Lucy at 8am on 19 July. They unexpectedly 'bumped' into a parked German convoy and drove through it, exchanging fire as they went. As McGuinn explained, 'It was too late to turn back so we decided to shoot our way through.' The jeep, which had engine trouble, could not exceed 30mph. A burst of enemy fire hit them as they passed the last vehicle, killing Bradford and a Maquis mechanic and wounding everyone else except McGuinn. He continues: 'We were just out of sight of the last truck when the jeep "packed in" ... I could hear the Germans running down the road towards me and I made in the direction of the woods with the two wounded survivors.' Two days later, after a nightmarish journey across a series of rivers, the wounded were taken to a secret Maquis hospital at Chateau Vermot. McGuinn returned to the fight.

Such episodes were not unusual. At Montigny, two weeks later, an SAS jeep drove into a German ambush. After restarting a stalled engine and clearing jammed guns, Captain Wellstead reported: 'By now, to keep the gun in action, I had to climb on to the bonnet of the vehicle and as we whistled flat out down the hill I managed to spray the hedges and discourage them a bit.'

Meanwhile, in the Maquis hospital, White was learning that it was no sanctuary. The headboard of his bed was riddled by German gunfire during a surprise attack. The casualties, new and old, were evacuated and the hospital then burned down by the enemy.

Reprisals of a savage kind were frequently extracted by the Wehrmacht after SAS attacks, both on French civilians and any SAS soldier taken prisoner. Nowhere was this more evident than in the aftermath of Operation 'Loyton' in the Vosges mountains on the border between France and Germany. As originally conceived, the operation should have started before D-Day. In fact, it did not begin until late August, by which time it had become a principal axis of German retreat and defence of the fatherland. It was, like most areas immediately to the rear of such a position, saturated by soldiers. The local Maquis were untrained, unarmed and riddled with Nazi informers. The result was that the teams from 2 SAS were harried night and day from one unsafe base to another and finally, in late September and early October, straggled back to Allied lines in small numbers. Two survivors buried their arms and dressed as women to elude capture.

One village, Moussey, fed and concealed the SAS throughout those unpleasant six weeks. The German revenge was to remove the entire male population — 210 men and boys — to concentration camps. Of the 70 who returned after the war, many died from the effects of starvation and torture. Of the 81 SAS men involved, 30 were either killed, taken prisoner or officially 'missing in action'. Most of these were shot by the Gestapo, some after barbaric torture.

Yet even 'Loyton' was not an absolute failure; numerous vehicles had been ambushed and railways cut. The greatest single coup was that of Major P. le Poer Power who, within 48 hours of landing in France, radioed details of an SS headquarters and a fuel dump containing three million litres of petrol. Both were destroyed by RAF bombers within two days. The attack on the headquarters killed 400 SS men as they paraded before moving out.

Parachute operations became all but impossible as the winter of 1944 set in. The Belgian SAS squadron and a detachment of French 4th Parachute Battalion performed 'useful reconnaissance' in jeeps and on foot in December and January, during the German offensive in the Ardennes. An operation planned for Norway was aborted because of bad weather. The Belgians and the two British SAS regiments were operating continuously as an advanced reconnaissance screen for the main Allied forces from the end of March 1945, after the Rhine crossing, until the end of the war in May. In Germany, the Regiment put the first soldiers into the port of Kiel, one of the many occasions when their early arrival was aimed at forestalling sabotage by the retreating Germans. Another task, during the final days of the conflict and for some time after, was the interrogation of known and suspected Nazis, many of whom were guilty of war crimes and were now trying to escape. A scheme that was planned, but dropped at the last moment, was to send SAS teams on rescue missions to Colditz high security prison. There, it was thought, British 'prominenten' prisoners related to the royal family might be used as hostages, or executed simply out of spite.

In Holland, men from both French battalions plus the Belgians were dropped in 50 small parties totalling 700 men. Their mission was to speed up the liberation of that country by harassing enemy communications, causing general confusion and preventing the demolition of important bridges. Some men, including the Belgian SAS, were at Arnhem. Later, men from 1 SAS were the first to liberate the walking skeletons of Belsen concentration camp in Germany itself.

Soon after the war, following a brief foray into Norway to supervise the surrender of thousands of German soldiers there, the French and Belgian units were formally incorporated into their own armies and the British regiments disbanded. When the SAS re-emerged, it was in another part of the world, in a totally different sort of conflict. More significantly, its rebirth marked a rebirth of Stirling's principle that small is elegant and cost-effective.

68. The SRS was taken by sea from Marro di Porco to a more formidable obstacle along the coast: the town of Augusta, defended by the Wehrmacht's Hermann Goering Panzer Division. The scene in Augusta's main street after the battle confirmed a report from the defenders, published in a German newspaper: 'We had suffered absolute hell from the RAF bombing and the accuracy of naval shelling, but it was the last straw when a British parachute regiment landed ... Machine-guns, artillery and mortars were turned on them but still they came on. Nothing could stop them.'

69-71. Out in the countryside, meanwhile, other SAS men were seizing positions on both sides of the line. One group found the wreckage of troop-carrying gliders, some full of dead British soldiers. Some of those who survived the landing had been shot in the back. Other gliders littered the harbour, still afloat as the amphibious invasion came in.

72, 73. Sicily was secured after 38 days' fighting. An unopposed landing on the Italian mainland at Taranto, coinciding with the Italian Government's surrender, was followed by stiff skirmishes inland by 2 SAS, then still in its infancy. The Regiment was used initially as a forward reconnaissance screen by the advancing Allied army. Meanwhile, SRS (1 SAS) was tasked to seize the port of Bagnara, behind enemy lines, in an amphibious operation. Elaborate preparations for such an operation included oblique air photographs (**72**) and carefully annotated maps (**73**). In spite of this, the Royal Navy landed the troops in error to the north of the town rather than the south. This created an unexpected opportunity. One of Mayne's troop commanders, Captain 'Pat' Riley, was told to climb cliffs to a point overlooking the town. From this position, Riley noted that German machine-gunners were in position, facing the other way. Riley's troop hit them from the rear,

killing some and taking prisoner 21 others. These were probably the first Germans captured in Italy. They were fresh from the Russian front. As the SRS men were hit by enemy shell fire, one prisoner, at some risk to himself, gave first-aid to one of his wounded captors. Soon after dawn, the SAS had occupied the town. Over the next two days, the Regiment repelled a series of counterattacks. Five SAS men and about twenty Germans died in these battles. But with local bridges seized intact by the SAS, the main Allied advance was accelerated and casualties reduced. The SAS then handed over the town to others and started training for the next operation.

74. While SRS (1 SAS) was reorganizing, men of 2 SAS were busy behind German lines in a series of guerrilla campaigns that continued until the end of the war. They sometimes operated independently of the partisans, like this team in action with a 3-inch mortar.

75. More frequently, 2 SAS supplied the partisans with weapons and trained and led them. Or, like these three soldiers parachuted into the Castino area, they might trudge through the mountains to bring a Vickers machine-gun into position to provide additional punch and give the partisans more confidence in fighting the Wehrmacht.

76, 77. As mutual confidence increased between partisans and SAS, so the soldiers were seen in towns as well as the mountains. In Castino village square, behind the local First World War memorial, an SAS team cleans and oils its weapons (**76**). Parachutes conceal boxes of ammunition and rations (left) to discourage theft. Elsewhere in the village, armed partisans — one wearing a bullet-proof pad on his chest — stroll past a Union Jack (**77**). The flag, a signal to avert possible attack by the RAF, is hastily pinned in position with a rock on each corner.

△75 ▽76 ▽77

△78

△79

△81

▽83

△80

△82 ▽84

78. The partisans of Alba were especially well equipped. They had a 'staff car', complete with safety chain in place of doors. Evacuation from the vehicle, and into the nearest ditch if they came under fire, was easier without doors. Here, the locals are seen with Captain Macdonald, a Canadian officer with 2 SAS (standing), as they take him on a reconnaissance mission.

79. In spite of its occasionally theatrical qualities, the Italian partisan campaign was real warfare — the casualties were real. The comparatively lucky ones were evacuated by air through the good offices of the SAS. Here, an RAF Lysander of the type that recovered agents from clandestine air strips inside hostile territory is used to lift out a severely wounded partisan shot in an engagement with Italians still loyal to fascism.

80-83. Soldiers of both the SRS (1 SAS) and 2 SAS finally met and fought together at Termoli in October 1943. In the town itself, the wreckage of a German Lancia lorry captured by the SAS and then destroyed by German gunners with a direct hit litters the street (**80**). A number of SRS men in the vehicle at the time were killed instantly. This distant photograph of Termoli station (**81**) was taken during the battle. Elsewhere on the same line, Roy Farran discovered that a railway engine and truck immediately in front of his position was loaded with high-explosive. The muzzle brake of a Sherman tank — its target was a sniper in a nearby cemetery — is just discernible in photograph **82**. With the battle finally over, the SAS survivors start to emerge from their foxholes (**83**). The Battle of Termoli was a desperate, epic affair in which SAS men often fought with weapons abandoned in panic by friend and foe alike. It accelerated sharply the Eighth Army advance and reduced potential casualties as a result. It was also memorable for an episode at the start of the German counterattack in which Mayne mischievously continued playing billiards on a table in a building that was now being bombarded by German shells. His fellow players became increasingly nervous. Watched anxiously by the Medical Officer, Captain Gunn, by Major Bill Fraser and Captain Pat Riley, Mayne coolly finished the game and returned to the battle as a messenger announced that German soldiers had reached an adjoining street. One spectator said later: 'It was like watching Drake play bowls, but this time the enemy were much closer.'

84. Before they left Termoli, en route for Scotland and Occupied France, these men of 2 SAS posed for the official war photographer, wearing freshly delivered trousers and a collection of collarless, civilian shirts. Subsequently, the censor laboriously erased the SAS cap badge. The leader of this group, Major Sandy Scratchley, DSO, MC, had served under David and Bill Stirling, and it was he who assisted his colourful Eighth Army friend, Roy Farran, to join the SAS.

△ 85

85, 86. Occupied France, 31 August 1944, and a battalion of élite Nazi SS soldiers is preparing to move out of its headquarters at the boys' school in Vincey, in the Vosges. Their rifles are stacked in neat pyramids in front of the building and the men lined up on parade when RAF fighter-bombers swoop in at low level, raking the area with machine-gun fire, bombing the buildings. These photographs, taken from the aircraft at the time, show (**85**) the school building on the left intact as the attack begins; the same building demolished, seconds later (**86**). The man who inspired the attack was Major P. le Poer Power of 2 SAS. With Lieutenant J. A. McGregor, DSO, and eight others, he had been parachuted by night into the wrong drop zone only three days before. The men hid in the woods until radio communications could be established with other SAS units. 'To employ my time when waiting', wrote Power, 'I asked the Maquis to get me all possible information of bombing targets, disposition of troops, etc. I selected as the two best bombing targets an SS HQ at Vincey and a dump of three million litres of petrol at Nomexy. Subsequent information proved that these targets had been bombed successfully. Four hundred SS were killed while parading to move out. The petrol was all destroyed and the glow of the fire could be seen on two successive nights.' Later, all the men on Operation 'Loyton' had narrow escapes. McGregor's report records some typical experiences: 'Sept. 26: We stayed at a farm and found Madame to be very courageous. Several times she fed us upstairs while there were six or seven Germans downstairs.

She also brought us up German cigarettes and fresh information of the American front line. Oct. 4: Waited hopefully in woods for 48 hours, watching Germans eating our anticipated food and digging machine-gun emplacements less than 20 yards away. Oct. 6: Tightened our belts and took Benzedrine. I decided as

△ 87   ▽ 89

▽ 88

△86

there were Germans in every house and we were considerably weakened by lack of food, we would cross the lines on the following day. Oct. 8: Crossed lines with 15 noisy Frenchmen, via Jeanmenil, map ref. V221712 to Rambervillers.'

87. In the village cemetery at Moussey, the centre of many of these operations, there is a permanent reminder of some of the men who died on them. Many others vanished without trace. The commemorative tablet reads: 'Here lie the bodies of officers, NCOs and soldiers of 2 SAS Regiment who, with three exceptions, were shot by the Germans in 1944 after they became prisoners of war: Lieutenant Castellain, killed in action, near Raon-l'Etape, 11 October; Lieutenant Silly, shot at Saint-Prayel, 22 October; Sergeant Lodge, killed by a bullet in the head at Moussey, 19 August; Sergeant Fitzpatrick, shot at Pexonne with Privates Conway and Elliott, 16 September; Sergeant Davies, shot in the woods at Moussey, c. 19 August; Privates Brown and Lewis, shot with an unknown Frenchman at Harcholet, 16 October; Private Casparovitch, accidentally killed at Moussey, 28 September; Private Johnston, killed in action near Fontenoy-la-Joute, 11 October.'

88, 89. On the advance into Holland in 1944, SAS soldiers were fighting behind German lines at Arnhem and, in a more shallow penetration, as a forward reconnaissance screen for the main Allied advance. The Regiment also took into custody some notorious Nazi collaborators. This woman (**88**), a Dutch suspect, was taken at Blerik. While the vehicle paused for a photographer

to record the event, her right hand tentatively fingered the escort's American M1 carbine. As the war moved into Germany itself, the Wehrmacht fought as hard as ever. During the battle for Gelsenkirchen near Essen, Sergeant A. Schofield and Trooper O. Jeavons (**89**) comprised one of several SAS teams given the difficult and dangerous job of killing snipers. Their jeep was equipped with one twin and one single Vickers machine-gun up front and a Lewis gun, under wraps, mounted at the rear. The removal of the radiator grille suggests that the vehicle had once carried a condenser for use in the Western Desert campaign.

90, 91. During the final stages of the conflict in Europe, the SAS had to become more accustomed to the symbolism of parades and other ceremonies than it had been in the past. Here (**90**), General Montgomery reviews French SAS men serving in the British Army in April 1944, a few months before D-Day. He talks to Colonel Durand, their commander. At that time the SAS was part of Airborne Forces, which included the Parachute Regiment, so Durand wears the red beret, Parachute Regiment cap badge, Airborne's Pegasus arm badge and French insignia of rank. On his chest are SAS wings awarded to men who had already been on operations. A more characteristic SAS occasion was this one in Norway (**91**). The Regiment's last military task before it was disbanded in 1945 was to disarm thousands of Wehrmacht soldiers in that country. When this troop was leaving, it said farewell to Norway with a ceremonial parade in jeeps on a provincial football pitch.

▽90

▽91

△92

△93

In 1947, two years after the Second World War, the SAS slipped back into the British Army through the back door, as a humble Territorial regiment composed of part-time reserve soldiers. It was called 21 SAS, and an existing unit, the Artists' Rifles, was linked with it. The Artists' Rifles, after it was raised in 1859, recruited such famous pre-Raphaelite painters as Millais and Holman Hunt. During the First World War, the Regiment was a 'nursery' for potential officers, one of whom was the poet Edward Thomas. Thomas, who knew England's footpaths better than most, served with the Artists as a navigation instructor with the rank of corporal, before he was commissioned as a gunner and killed in a forward observation post at Arras in 1917. The first Commanding Officer of 21 SAS (Artists' Rifles) was Colonel Brian Franks, who had led 2 SAS in Occupied France. Many of his 'weekend' soldiers were, in fact, old comrades-in-arms.

Barely a year after this resurrection, and thousands of miles away in the Malayan jungle, Communist guerrillas operating from carefully prepared secret bases and using arms originally supplied by Britain to fight the Japanese, began a campaign of terrorism. One of their leaders, Chin Peng, had just received an OBE for his part in the Second World War. Caught off balance, the British countered with a defensive, passive strategy of road-blocks, guarded convoys and the like. The heart of the conflict, however, was in the jungle. The first people to pursue this logic, and the enemy, were members of an ad hoc group known as 'Ferret Force'. The 'Ferret Force' operations uncovered twelve elaborate jungle camps, but because the valuable talent tied up in the Force was needed elsewhere, the unit was disbanded.

The war — for that was what it rapidly became — went the Communists' way for a time. Then, Mike Calvert, a tough soldier who had commanded the SAS brigade during its last days in Europe, and who was now based in Hong Kong, was given the job of producing a detailed analysis of the Malayan problem. Calvert himself was an experienced jungle guerrilla. Six energetic months later, he produced a number of ideas, including the creation of a force able to sweat it out in the 'ulu' (jungle), living hard for much longer than was then regarded as normal. The new force would have to wait, and wait, and finally ambush the enemy. He also suggested that the new unit should be known as the Malayan Scouts (SAS).

Calvert could not be as selective as the Regiment had been in the past, and would be in future. He was limited to the volunteers he acquired on the spot; some were superb soldiers, but others were cowboys. This variegated group formed up as 'A' Squadron and from Britain came 'B' Squadron, a group of volunteers from 21 SAS. Many were war veterans; few knew the jungle. Later, Rhodesian volunteers created 'C' Squadron, and they were succeeded in Malaya by the New Zealand SAS.

Training for the Malayan Scouts was as hard and unorthodox as the jungle itself, where the unwary might die of any one of a catalogue of diseases, to say nothing of such hazards as poisonous snakes or trees that collapse, crushing the sleeper beneath. Education in what were called 'training-operations' could reduce such natural hazards. To

△ **94**

92, 93. The Malayan war was unlike any the SAS had fought before. The hit-and-run guerrilla tactics of the desert and Europe — in which everything happened at high speed — were replaced by a relentless, plodding trek on foot through dense jungle. There was a change of role to accompany this change of pace: the enemy now was the guerrilla and the SAS had turned from poacher to gamekeeper. Sometimes both sides used the same camp sites in turn during their tortuous game of blind man's bluff. The action, when it came, was often one-to-one, since only the lead scout in a patrol might actually see, and be seen by, the opposition. So it was a highly personal combat. Early recruits to the Malayan Scouts, therefore, learned to stalk one another, using high powered air rifles firing darts not likely to kill, but sufficient to cause painful minor wounds. The face was protected with a fencing mask, as a gesture to training safety (**92**). As a gesture to reality, hand grenades were carried on waist belts (**93**). Sometimes they were primed, ready to use, sometimes not.
94. Each team, before it entered the jungle, had to become familiar with the weapons it would use. These included pump-action shotguns, whose spread of shot in dense undergrowth could be deadly at 25 yards, and the lightweight Owen submachine-gun, shown here in the hands of volunteers from the New Zealand SAS.

prepare for the uniquely personal warfare of jungle combat, Calvert's men learned to stalk one another with air rifles. As a concession to safety, they were allowed to wear fencing masks. They also hurled live grenades from the uncertain cover of drainage ditches. In fact, much of their small arms training — like that of 2 SAS in its formative days in Algeria — made liberal use of live ammunition. For some palates the Malayan Scouts' discipline was as casual as the risk-taking and, after Calvert's retirement due to ill-health, many of the original Scouts were returned to their units as men not up to SAS standards.

It should be set on record, however, that the Scouts also achieved much. They proved that prolonged jungle operations were possible using supplies dropped in by parachute. They exploited the shotgun as a military weapon in a twilit world where 1,800 man-hours were expended for one, fleeting close-range contact with the enemy. A typical pioneer of that time was Lieutenant Michael Sinclair-Hill, whose patrol emerged from the endless, claustrophobic gloom of undergrowth after 103 days. Gallantry awards to the Scouts from 1950 to 1952 testify that these men were not all 'beards and bullshit'. Later, the SAS also launched a 'hearts-and-minds' campaign among Malaya's numerous aboriginal tribes, which were being intimidated into supporting the Communists, most of whom were towns-people and ethnic Chinese. The use of medical aid as a means of winning friends was also recommended in those early days by Major P. D. R. Williams-Hunt, government Adviser on Aborigines, who pointed out: 'Aborigines prefer things that can be rubbed on externally rather than injections or

pills and if these are in gay colours, like gentian violet, so much the better. Supplies of drugs must not be left with the Aborigines.' The use of such medicines — as well as more potent penicillin — by SAS 'bush doctors', in addition to the simple presence of the soldiers in a few areas, started a long process in an attempt to occupy popular sympathy in Malaya rather than territory.

In 1952, the SAS pioneered the hazardous technique of parachuting into the jungle. In theory, the soldier guided his canopy into trees that would first snag it and then support it. He might still be 100ft above ground, suspended in the harness. A rope was carried to enable him to complete the journey. In practice, most drops produced serious injuries, including broken backs, and sometimes injury or death resulted from the use of the rope. Such were the risks that the technique was abandoned in exercises, and used only in necessary operations against a real enemy.

In the same year the Malayan Scouts formally became 22 Special Air Service Regiment: a unique military innovation in that a regular, full-time force was the offspring of a reserve, part-time Territorial regiment. John Woodhouse, one of Calvert's best recruits, later to command 22 SAS, returned to Britain to set up a full-time selection and training course. The SAS was now back in business, just seven years after being officially laid to rest. Increasingly, it attracted veteran fighters from 1 SAS, such as John Cooper, as well as other irregular warfare experts who had learned their business with the Long Range Desert Group, the Commandos, the Special Operations Executive and elsewhere. One of these was Major Dare Newell, OBE, an old SOE hand with experience in Albania and Japanese-occupied Malaya, who later became the SAS Regimental Adjutant.

The type of war now being fought in the jungle required new skills, fresh talent and the adaptation of existing techniques. In some cases, the three elements came together. Iban trackers from Sarawak who liked to collect parts of their dead enemy's anatomy, formed a Ranger unit to work with the SAS and from them, as well as hard experience, some SAS men learned to become excellent trackers themselves. Long-range Morse signalling was more important than ever, but in this environment, some signallers found it expedient to learn to use a bow and arrow in order to launch an aerial through the jungle canopy and ensure reliable transmission. Some innovations worked, some did not. Helicopters could not always land in tight jungle clearings so the SAS learned to abseil into the jungle from ropes fixed to the aircraft. Another scheme, to use elephants as a mobile base camp, came to grief when the selected elephants declined to go where the SAS wanted. Beyond all else, the greatest single innovation was the adaptation of European soldiers to the extraordinary environment of the jungle. Throughout a twelve-week operation, the average SAS trooper would retain, as if he had toothache, the awareness of the proximity of his enemy.

He found the 'bandits' camps, often freshly evacuated, quite regularly, but usually the weeks would pass and the operation would end without contact. Meanwhile, the front of his mind was engaged with the question of his own survival; with fatigue; the endless rain; the sudden brilliance of a shaft of sunlight and butterflies; tree felling to create drop zones; pursuit of fish with hand grenades; avoidance of an accidental shot which might kill a comrade; awareness that some tribes kept pigs as pets — even suckled them when young — and that the animals were therefore untouchable; the snake in the bed; the wait for the re-supply air drop and the disappointment when the package with Naafi stores and letters from home was swept away over a waterfall. Even the letter, when it arrived, was often a 'Dear John . . .' For the soldier packing up his gear in pouring rain, itching from insect bites and scabes or both, facing another day slithering over bamboo-clad mountain or waist-deep swampland, very small things could make a big difference to the day. The Day. Yesterday was finished; tomorrow would probably be worse. Today mattered enormously. The SAS men made it tolerable with mordant humour. David Kirby, one of the few National Service conscripts to serve with the Regiment, kept a detailed diary of his Malayan operations which reflects this.

'Saturday, 15 September, 1956: Started our patrol at high

speed. I was near the end of the line so had to run far too much. After an hour and a half we reached an old base camp. Fond hopes of stopping there soon shattered. On we went, nipping back and forth across the river, which grew rapidly in size. Apart from river risks, the only interest was fending off thousands of leeches, which galloped up my trousers in families, one big one and assorted little ones, and in droves.' (According to Regimental folklore, another squadron ordered hundreds of male contraceptives to protect the most sensitive area from the leeches depredations.)

On 9 November his patrol encountered other teams from 'D' Squadron. They marched in, led by Woodhouse. 'They looked shattered . . . One lad was against a tree asleep. He said later he was surprised when we woke him. He dreamt he was still marching!'

Kirby, the patrol medic, and a qualified architect, had the job of building a lavatory wherever they stopped. 'Monday, 10 December: Spent the morning building the privy — the medic's job. It will look good when I apply for a post: "Experience, public conveniences and small dwellings throughout Northern Malaya".'

The Malayan war, euphemistically described as an 'Emergency', lasted eleven years until 1959. It was won by a combination of land, sea and air forces, and through the control of food and people, as well as the jungle pursuit of an enemy who was an elusive, skilful will-o'-the-wisp. The Gurkhas apart, however, it was the SAS that stayed with the campaign the longest. (Jungle experience is still a basic part of regimental training.) Gradually, as those years passed, the Communists were forced to defend their bases rather than launch attacks on roads and plantations. Then, as the exhausting process of food control — including body searches of those leaving defended villages — took effect, so the guerrillas had to concentrate on simple survival. To eat, they now had to grow their own food, which necessitated clearing areas of jungle to allow sunlight to nurture the crops. Such settlements rapidly fell victim to air reconnaissance.

One of the last guerrilla hunts, in a coastal swamp region of Selangor, was launched by 'D' Squadron in February 1958. A total of 37 men led by Harry Thompson parachuted into a 180 square-mile search area to capture or kill two groups of terrorists led by Ah Hoi, whose nickname, 'Baby Killer', resulted from his public execution of a pregnant woman. One of those who jumped on this operation, Trooper Mulcahy, broke his back in a catastrophic tree landing. The initial search for Ah Hoi was led by Captain Peter de la Cour de la Billière. For ten days he and his troops followed a river 'bank', much of it submerged, through the swamp. Their first clue was a collection of turtle shells, the débris of a recent dinner. Another patrol, led by Sergeant Sandilands, was also approaching the centre of the swamp on a different axis and moving at night. At dusk, this group spotted two of the enemy across open water. The sergeant and a corporal floated a log in front of them, across the 70 yards between them and their quarry. At 50 yards they opened fire, killing one man. The other fled, leaving a bloody trail. The military cordon round the area was tightened and intensified. About 20 days after the operation began, Ah Hoi sent out a messenger — a woman — to parley and finally negotiate surrender.

Back in Britain, meanwhile, the great defence review of 1957, which ended National Service and amalgamated many famous regiments, left the SAS intact. However, it was clear that the continued existence of a full-time SAS regiment was not yet guaranteed. As long as the Malayan conflict lasted, then 22 SAS had a raison d'être, but it still had to prove its relevance to British post-war strategy outside the jungle. With the end of the Malayan campaign in sight, the SAS was once again fighting for its own political survival within a defence bureaucracy that only dimly understood the Regiment's potential value.

◁95 △96 ▽97

95-97. Simply by being in the jungle, the SAS maintained constant pressure on the Communists. Each side knew that the other was always there, and both were under stress as a result. The war would be decided when one side or the other cracked under the strain. But, before it could apply that pressure, the Regiment's teams had to be moved into operational areas and extracted again after three months to hand over to the next squadron. Such mobility was itself a strategic trump card, but the landing zones (**95**) were dangerously tight, and those soldiers who went in by helicopter did not always make it (**96**), some of the Regiment's best men, including Major Harry Thompson, were lost in helicopter crashes. This pilot (**97**) was lucky: trying to evacuate an SAS casualty, he caught a tail rotor on a log. The machine was then stranded for several days until spares and a mechanic could be flown in.

△98　　　　　　△99　　　　　　△100　▽101

▽102　　　　　　　　　　　　　　　　103▷

98-103. The other fast route into deep jungle was by parachute. In the 1950s the British soldier still depended on a single, main parachute, back-packed and detached on landing by hitting a quick-release box on the chest. This SAS jumper (**98**), his beret tucked inside the chest harness, carries much of his equipment inside his parachute smock, resting on his stomach. The valise (left) holding a rifle or Bren machine-gun is strapped to his leg and released on a rope before he touches down. The rope (or webbing) was also used for the climb from the tree-tops to the ground. In **99** an officer in training is using webbing in a demonstration of this manoeuvre. When it malfunctioned, the webbing/rope caused fatalities. In stifling heat, the men don their kit (**100**). This was usually followed by an exhausting wait while parachute instructors checked that all was in order (**101**). The men emplane (**102**), led by an officer whose helmet bears the Artists' Rifles badge of 21 SAS. This was the moment when the adrenalin started to flow. Inside the RAF transport (**103**), the men's static lines are hooked up to cables.

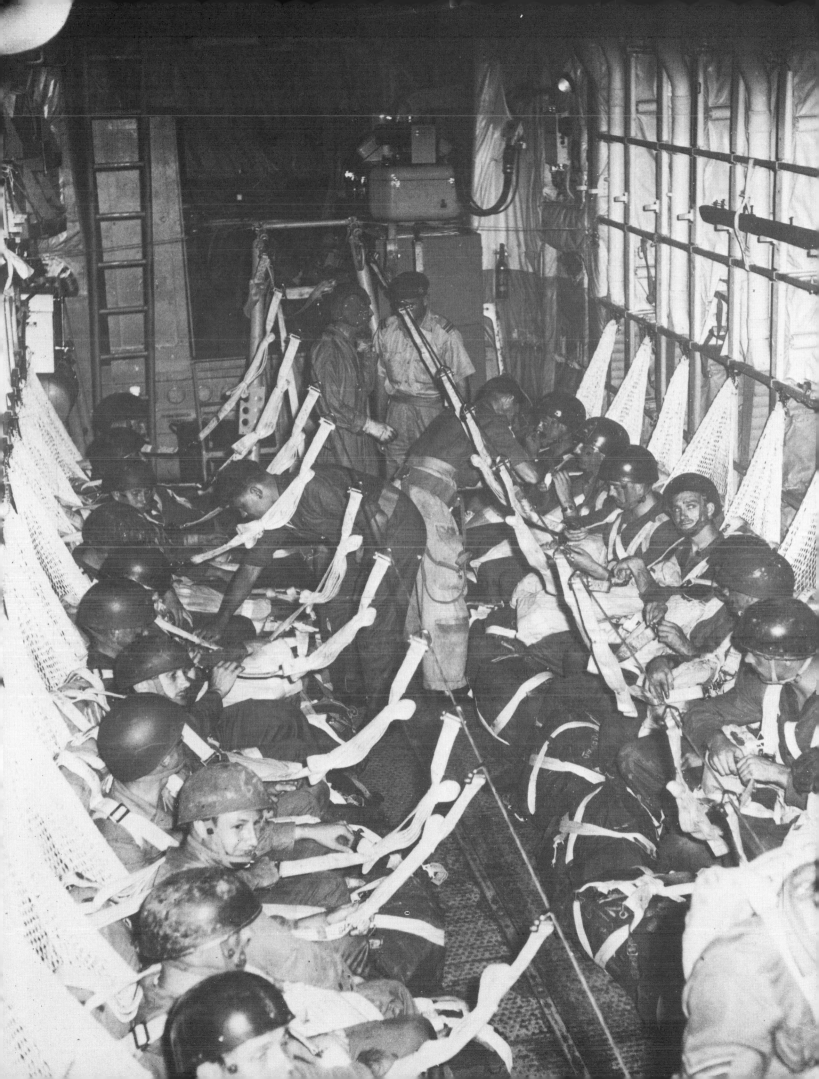

104-106. As they jump — through a door now, rather than a hole in the floor — the static line opens the parachute. It usually worked (**104**), but the worst, the tree landing, was yet to come. For Sergeant Hanna (**105**), all went well. For Trooper Mulcahy (**106**), the adventure ended with a broken back.

▽104   △105   △106

△107

△108 ▽110

△109   ▽111   ▽112

107-112. Once in the jungle, most movement was on foot, carrying on one's back almost everything required for survival. The four-man patrol was still the basic SAS unit (**107**) for operational forays from a base camp, but for many marches across country, Malayan aboriginal tribesmen were hired as additional porters, while Iban and Dyak trackers, imported from Sarawak, might also be included in the march. Here (**108**), such a mixed force moves off. One SAS soldier (third from right) moves in bare feet. Getting wet — for there was no route that did not involve crossing rivers (**109**) — was part of the day's routine. Fighting patrols, such as this group of New Zealanders (**110**), often followed rivers if it was quicker and left no tell-tale footprint to be identified by the human enemy. The leeches were another matter. For the last lap out of the 'ulu', some men — like these from 'D' Squadron coming out by rail at the end of an operation commanded by Major Dare Newell — there was even the novel comfort of travel on wheels (**111**). Occasionally, when long distance travel back to base or the helicopter rendezvous was necessary, and the river was going the right way, it was possible to travel by raft (**112**).

113-120. In reality, the soldier's life in the jungle is not like that of a Tarzan movie. It has its own rhythm, a strange mixture of domesticity without women or children, and preparedness for instant combat. Weapons have to be dried, cleaned, oiled; shelters ('bashas') prepared; ailments — particularly malaria — forestalled with daily paludrin tablets; clothes washed; food cooked. In the jungle, none of these tasks are ordinary and prosaic. They are exotic skills; rituals which mark the passing of the day. On the march, the 'brew-up' (tea-making) is an event of such significance that it is photographed more frequently than combat itself. This tea-break (**113**) reflects the temporary relief from the sweaty agony of the march. Work to clear parachute drop zones or helicopter landing zones (**114**) might take days, but the alternative to aerial resupply will be, at best, acute hunger. The drop, when it comes in, often goes tantalisingly astray (**115**). One soldier makes a novel but unsuccessful attempt to dislodge the parachute with bow and arrow (**116**). When the gear is eventually recovered with the aid of aboriginal tree climbers, there is the task of sorting it all out (**117**). Occasionally, there are rest days: time to read, write and reflect, pump-action shotgun to hand (**118**). Others, restless with boredom, go out and catch something (**119**) or, as in the case of this python (**120**), convert it into an article of clothing.

121-124. Apart from simply being there in the jungle, as a constant presence, the SAS's greatest intangible weapon in this strange war was its ability to make friends. There were at least three racially and culturally distinctive types of aborigine in Malaya at this time, who had to be won over, as well as allies such as Gurkhas, Iban and Dyak tribesmen, some of them headhunters, brought as trackers from Sarawak. Contact might be made in unexpectedly small ways. This soldier (**121**) shared his cigarettes. Fortunately, his companion did not come from the Semai Senoi tribe, within which the shared cigarette, between man and woman, binds them in marriage. Respect for their allies' martial skills (**122**), medical treatment combined with social calls (**123**), or earthy humour (**124**) were collectively a potent weapon of diplomacy.

△113

△114

▽117

▽121

▽122

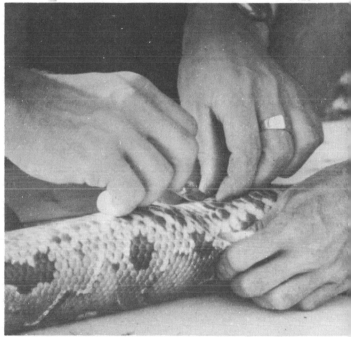

▽118   ▽119   △115 △116   ▽120

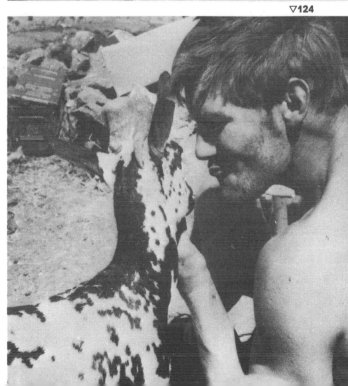

▽123   ▽124

125, 126. There were also enemies. Some, like Communist guerrilla leader Chin Peng photographed here (**125**) at an unsuccessful conference to end the conflict peacefully are well known. Others, like this defiant woman (**126**) were identified only when cordon, search and starvation forced them out of the jungle. The corpses of enemy dead had to be carried out for identification. It was one of the most distasteful tasks an SAS soldier faced.

127-130. The sharp end of this war was the deadly game of hide-and-seek, which rapidly accelerated once 'contact' — a short, intensive brush — with the enemy had been made. For some, the painful patience of waiting in silent ambush (**127**) while being eaten by a variety of insects was the order of the day. For others, like this New Zealand team using tracker dogs (**129**) mobility was stepped up sharply. The 'bandits' responded by running dogs ahead of their patrols, to give them warning. Such a search took the Regiment into hidden caves (**128**) and clearings where there were traces of a Communist camp (**130**).

131, 132. Often, the search yielded nothing. After three months, these soldiers are told that they are being brought out. One man orders a haircut (**131**), another takes a shave. Almost everyone gets spruced up, and a little edgy, as 'D' (for departure) day gets closer (**132**). The 'chopper' is on its way. It will be odd to go to bed without a gun.

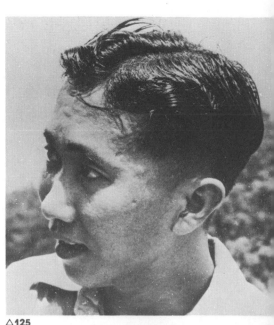

△125

◁127　△128　▽130

△126

△129 ▽131 ▽132

Jebel Akhdar, Aden, Borneo, 1959–1967
Minimum force

Between 1959 and 1967, the SAS fought three 'low intensity' campaigns of which the British public knew little and cared less; campaigns which, nevertheless, had important implications for Britain's long-term military strategy and which assured the regular 22 SAS Regiment of a permanent place in the British Army. Those campaigns were the short, successful mountain war of Jebel Akhdar in northern Oman; the more protracted jungle conflict in Borneo; and the bitter mixture of urban terrorism in Aden city combined with the pitiless mountain warfare in the arid Radfan hills.

'Jebel Akhdar', translated from the Arabic, means 'Green Mountain'. It rises 7,000ft straight out of the desert and had not been conquered for 1,000 years when the SAS, most of it still in Malaya, was given the task of climbing its sheer face to end a rebellion against Britain's ally the Ruler of Oman. The suppression of the rebellion had to be achieved quickly, quietly and preferably with no casualties because of anti-British sentiment in the Middle East after the 1956 Suez débâcle and the geopolitics of the United Nations. One officer involved, Colonel Tony Jeapes, later described how this apparently impossible mission was accomplished. 'After a feint squadron night attack in the north to draw the enemy's attention and reserves in that direction, the two squadrons of SAS climbed the Jebel in one night from the south. It was a hard, long climb and only just accomplished. The heading troops dropped their bergen rucksacks and pushed on carrying only their rifles and belt equipment to reach the crest just at first light. Had the squadrons been caught in the low ground still climbing up those bare slopes at dawn it might have been a different story.'

Only one SAS soldier, Corporal 'Duke' Swindells, MM, was killed. The campaign lasted a few short months, compared with the long war which would occur later in southern Oman's Dhofar mountains, yet it had great political ramifications. It influenced the government of the day to adopt a strategy of using military 'firemen', based in Britain, to protect interests in the Third World. It demonstrated, as vividly as the Iranian Embassy siege in London years later, the ability of the SAS to adapt instantly to a totally new climate and different style of warfare. It went a long way towards consolidating the Regiment's permanence, rather than a reputation as a good jungle force whose value was limited to the expiring Malayan conflict.

The wars in Borneo and South Arabia were more serious. The first of these conflicts lasted from 1962 until 1966; the second, from 1964 to 1967. For much of the time the SAS was involved in both campaigns simultaneously. A squadron would serve for up to five months in Borneo, return to Britain for a brief period of leave and retraining and then fight in South Arabia for four months. This was a stunning exhibition of endurance as well as military skill. One veteran of the period, asked to compare the baking heat of Radfan with the foetid undergrowth of Borneo, said he regarded the jungle as 'a very gracious living'.

The Borneo troubles began with a local, internal insurrection against the Ruler of Brunei. In Brunei, it was rapidly suppressed, but it escalated into a war waged by Indonesia across a long, unmarked, mountainous frontier against Malaysian Borneo. Malaya, now independent, was an ally and Britain went to her aid. Superficially, this campaign had much in common with the Malayan conflict of the fifties. Both were fought in the jungle to defend a political status quo. In both, the SAS had to win the confidence of uncommitted tribesmen, many of whom had never seen a European before. But there were also important differences. In Malaya, the opposition was an irregular if well disciplined guerrilla force with no back door to friendly territory. In Borneo, the enemy was a regular army launched from bases on its own sovereign territory. Unlike Malaya, where the British sought to arrest or kill the guerrillas, Borneo required a much more subtle response. This was to deter the Indonesian Government without provoking it to a larger, more ambitious level of violence; a finely-tuned use of force with as much diplomatic input as military knuckle. The world of the SAS was changing and the most profound change was towards a doctrine of limited force applied with surgical exactness.

The first step was to spread out the men of the Regiment in twos and fours in border villages, to make friendly contact with the tribesmen. Once that confidence had been won, vital intelligence started to flow, for no-one can move through the jungle for long without leaving some trace as obvious to a native as a traffic signal in a city. An alien boot print would have been enough. In fact, the Indonesians tended to use those jungle highways, the rivers, too freely for their own good. When they did take to the jungle, it was often to leave an easily-followed spoor of cigarette packages and other garbage. When these routes were identified, the SAS would watch them silently and give early warning of approaching Indonesian patrols. As soon as the enemy entered Malaysian territory, they would be ambushed by Gurkhas and other fighting forces delivered to the scene by helicopter. From stopping them on the border, the SAS, backed up by Gurkhas, went on to hit the Indonesians on their own territory, between their bases and the frontier. Always on these cross-border jobs (known as 'Claret' operations) force was applied selectively, causing enough punishment to demoralize the front-line Indonesians but not wreaking so much havoc as to cause them massive loss of face. Publicly, the British said virtually nothing about their military successes. The conflict was blandly described as 'Confrontation'.

To ensure that the sensitive process of border crossing did not blow back in Britain's face, SAS men carried Armalite rifles (which were not then issued to the British Army as a whole), wore non-regulation boots, carried no personal identification, and adopted a policy known as 'shoot-and-scoot'. It was a style of warfare that required men to move at a painfully cautious pace. Sometimes, only five or ten minutes in any half-hour were spent on the move, with the other twenty minutes devoted to sitting and listening. Conversation, when it was permitted, was conducted in whispers. Some SAS soldiers, when first back in Britain,

133-135. Scepticism, an SAS characteristic, is written on the faces of men being briefed on Christmas Day 1958 for the forthcoming assault on the 7,000ft high plateau of Jebel Akhdar (**133**). Top secret plans concerning the attack route were deliberately leaked to Arab muleteers in the knowledge that they would be relayed to the enemy. They were, and the defenders were fooled into concentrating their forces in the wrong place. Meanwhile, the real assault went in with SAS officers initially keeping a close eye on mules and muleteers (**134**). On a few rebel outposts that were manned, the opposition fought bravely and paid with their lives (**135**). One Arab, according to Colonel Jeapes, 'did a spectacular Hollywood-style death dive over a sheer cliff' rather than surrender.

△**133** ▽**134** ▽**135**

could not easily rid themselves of the habit. The nervous strain, even for these men, was enormous.

Though the SAS was not in search of combat — except when its men led Gurkha fighting patrols to their targets — there were many occasions when the two- and four-man teams did have to shoot their way out of trouble. One well documented case involved a patrol from 'D' Squadron in February 1965. Trooper Thompson, his thigh shattered by a burst of Indonesian fire from a thicket of bamboo, shot one of the enemy and then crawled back 1,000 yards towards his own side. The journey lasted 36 hours before he was found. Meanwhile, he applied a tourniquet to the wound and used morphia to deaden the pain. His sergeant, 'Geordie' Lillico, was wounded as gravely; he also treated his own injuries and hid almost among the Indonesians searching for him. He, too, was recovered by a British helicopter after about 36 hours. Both men received gallantry awards.

As time passed in this deadly little war, the expansionist aims of the Indonesian leader, Achmed Sukarno, became less and less credible. The cost in blood rose steadily. The Indonesians signed a peace agreement with Malaysia, ending the war — Britain's best camouflaged victory.

In South Arabia, meanwhile, the SAS was fighting another, very different war. A rising tide of Arab nationalism, backed by Soviet support for 'liberation' movements outside the Warsaw Pact countries, provoked an anti-colonial guerrilla war in the sheikhdoms whose rulers' credibility depended upon British muscle. In the sprawling urban slums of Aden, the liberators adopted the methods of terrorism, including the murder of other nationalists with whom they disagreed. Some British men dug themselves in for a prolonged struggle, but in London, successive governments set targets for self-government and then for a total British evacuation. This was interpreted in South Arabia as abdication. Since the existing rulers now enjoyed no apparent legitimacy, the stage was set for defections from the Federal Regular Army, and for military defeat. The SAS, like other security forces, was defending a lost cause.

The Regiment's involvement in South Arabia began sensationally. In April 1964, less than a year after a grenade attack on the British governor had triggered the Emergency, 'A' Squadron was sent to the remote military air base at Thumier, near the Radfan rebels' mountain stronghold on the Yemeni border. The soldiers' families thought that 'A' Squadron was exercising on Salisbury Plain. Their first information to the contrary was a press report — the more horrific because it was true — that Captain Robin Edwards and Trooper J. N. Warburton had been killed in action . . . and that the bodies had been beheaded.

Edwards's men had been the front runners in a punitive operation against the hardy hillmen, who knew their mountains stone by stone. The patrol had set off on a night march to enable the SAS to provide a safe drop zone for incoming Parachute Regiment soldiers. The patrol went tragically wrong. One man became sick early in the march and, instead of reaching the objective by dawn, the patrol had to take refuge at first light in a crude, stonewalled goat pen. By mid-morning they were surrounded, and the ensuing gun battle lasted all day. Edwards and Warburton were killed as the patrol tried to break out at dusk. The survivors marched on into the gloom, increasingly hazed and disoriented through lack of water but still fighting off tribesmen who followed them down the trail.

Thereafter, the Regiment was regularly engaged in undercover work in the Radfan mountains and the alleyways of urban Aden. On the hills, an SAS team would land with other troops but remain as an observation post after the rest had been withdrawn by helicopter. From their mountain eyries, and surviving immobile with a minimum of water in 120°F temperatures, the SAS men directed artillery fire and air strikes on the rebels. The tribesmen, who could not understand the uncanny accuracy of these bombardments, believed that the British had guns 'with eyes which seek you out wherever you go'. In and around Aden city, SAS men dressed as Arabs, carried weapons such as the heavy 9mm Browning pistol under their robes, and intercepted terrorists. Wherever possible, they took these men alive for interrogation. By now, terrorists caught in the act were almost the only source of hard information about the secret Arab armies. The original sources of such knowledge — European and Arab special branch men — had been assassinated.

Britain abandoned South Arabia in 1967. The last man out of the turbulent Radfan area was an SAS officer, who remained, ostensibly as a civilian technician, to advise the emerging army of South Yemen about the administration of the Thumier military base and airport. The new state, the People's Democratic Republic of Yemen, rapidly became a drab Soviet satellite and anything but democratic. It also became the launch pad for Russian adventures across the Red Sea into Somalia and Ethiopia, as well as a base for a new guerrilla war against the British in southern Oman.

136-138. The contrasting terrain of the Radfan mountains of South Arabia (**136**) and the Borneo jungle (**137**) in which the SAS was simultaneously engaged during the 1960s. In both places, Royal Navy helicopters flew the Regiment on many hazardous missions, like that depicted in the ultimate jungle flying photograph (**138**).

△136   ▽137   ▽138

139-143. The trip to one of the hill outposts was invariably tense and noisy. Here (**139**), SAS officers armed with American Armalite M16 rifles argue tactics. One of their troopers is alone with his thoughts about what lies ahead. Some hill outposts, such as this one (**140**), had heavily fortified camps including a helicopter pad on the summit. The drop could be anything from an emergency abseil descent with only a rifle and belt kit (**141**) or a more leisurely abseil into dense bush with equipment (**142**) to a friendly reception by elaborately tatooed aborigines (**143**). Either way, it is a long way from Hereford. By the time they returned there, some SAS soldiers were tatooed as decoratively as the aborigines.

△139 ▽140

△141   △142 ▽143

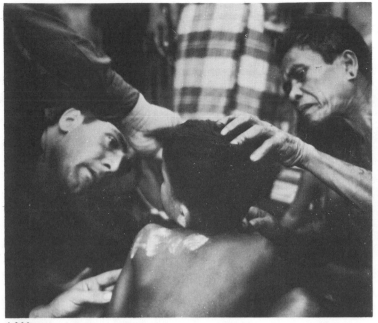

△144

△145

144-149. For men beginning their four- or five-month stint along a 700-mile front, life in the jungle settled into a familiar rhythm of local medical care (**144**), socializing with the locals (**145-147**), and jungle patrols by canoe (**148**) and on foot (**149**).

▽**148**　　　　　　△**146**　　　　　△**147**　　　　▽**149**

△152

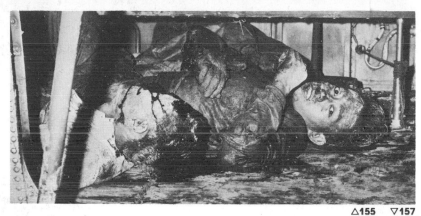

△155   ▽157

150-157. The enemy were the regular Indonesian Army, seen here preparing for the next attack from bases just across the border (**150**). They practise fieldcraft while carrying a British weapon, the Sten sub-machine-gun (**151**). The British were often armed with the more powerful American M16 Armalite. When contact occurred between the two, it happened suddenly and quickly. Here (**152**), the camera catches the speed with which SAS soldiers react to un-expected targets. The rivers are the highways of the jungle but also, as open space surrounded by cover, deadly dangerous. In **153** the SAS are the river-bank predators; in **154,** the prey. On the Indonesian side of the border, the policy was one of 'shoot-and-scoot'. An encounter on friendly territory often meant that the enemy dead had to be evacuated for identifica-tion (**155**). Indonesian infil-trators were ambushed with explosive traps as well as small arms. Here (**156**), such an ambush is being constructed. A patrol, at the end of an exhausting march back, faced the rituals of instant debriefing by an SAS officer, the comfort of the first cigarette, the chore of unloading magazines (**157**). After an operation the men's faces are unshaven; their eyes heavy with fatigue.

△158

△159 ▽160

▽161

158-161. As in so many SAS campaigns, the helicopter was the daily work-horse. In Radfan, the risk of landing was too great, so the men abseiled down a rope at high speed (**158**). On other occasions, the helicopter could actually land in the wilderness, as in this photograph of 'A' Squadron disembarking (**159**). The main base for the Radfan operations was Habilayn, a desolate airstrip near the border with North Yemen (**160**). It was from a tent here that SAS officers coordinated a series of air strikes by RAF Hunter jets in a desperate endeavour to relieve the pressure on the Edwards patrol, cut off and surrounded in the nearby hills. While the helicopter returned to the comparative comfort and security of a base like Habilayn, the patrol would begin the long, wearing task of survival in hostile mountains (**161**).

△162

△163

△165

△166 ▽167

162, 163. Once in the hills, the patrol's first priority was to gain the nearest summit before first light. To be caught below the guns of the Radfan tribesmen was as good as a death warrant. Here (**162**), the men scramble to reach their new observation post in time. They may then spend days in baking heat, listening, watching or, screened by a strip of hessian, simply sleeping (**163**). Even in sleep, this soldier's arm remains firmly crooked round his rifle. The photograph of an unarmed SAS man in an operational theatre is very rare indeed.

164-166. Before the campaign in South Arabia became a lost cause, not all contact between the SAS and the tribespeople was hostile. In 1964, 'D' Squadron took sixteen of its 'bush doctors', some capable of minor surgery, on training in the mountains of Fadhli State where this soldier (**164**) was photographed sharing a 'brew-up' with one of the locals. On more formal occasions, such as feasts given by tribal leaders (**165**), boots were removed but, as usual, weapons were kept to hand. Among a martial people, the expertise of men such as this SAS officer, giving an impromptu lecture to local sheikhs about mortar bombs, was respected. Weapons were a favourite topic (**166**).

167, 168. As the campaign ground on towards its bitter end, the British were fighting not just in what was to emerge as the Soviet satellite People's Democratic Republic of South Yemen, but also fending off the growing threat from Marxist revolutionaries to the neighbouring British ally of Oman. In 1966, during the final year of the British presence in Aden, 'B' Squadron of 22 SAS Regiment formed the spearhead of a cordon-and-search operation at Hauf, near the border with Oman (**167**). Though many of the guerrillas slipped through the net, the haul of weapons (**168**) was impressive. Later, however, these would be replaced by much more modern Soviet equipment including 122mm rocket launchers, which would be fired across the border at the SAS as they fought another hard mountain war in the southern Omani province of Dhofar.

△164 ▽168

Dhofar, 1970–1976
Persuasion and firepower

The fourteen-year conflict between the absolute monarchy of Oman and its left-wing opponents was Britain's last colonial war. At a time when Britain had already dismantled her empire, she made a unique exception in the case of Oman. There, she stood her ground, fought and won. The reason was Oman's unique importance to all Western economies. The Sultanate controls the Musandam Peninsular and therefore the Strait of Hormuz through which passes, on its way out of the Gulf, about 50 per cent of the West's crude oil. Oman was never a colony in the strict sense of the word, but a protected monarchy. Its disciplined army of Arabs, Baluchi mercenaries and others was officered by the British; its air force pilots drawn from the RAF; and its civil experts recruited from London. As a

British minister (Julian Amery) once put it, 'We give the Sultan help; we sometimes give him advice; but we do not give him orders.' Yet, historically, the Sultan depended almost entirely for his security on British money, ingenuity and muscle.

The system was only as good as the ruling sultan. From 1962, when the first guerrilla land mines signalled the start of the war, until 1970 the ruler was the aged and despotic Sa'id bin Taimur. His intolerance and cruelty fuelled the rebellion more effectively than the Marxism absorbed by Dhofari guerrilla leaders from South Yemen (PDRY), Russia or China. By the time bin Taimur was deposed by his only son, Sultan Qaboos — a Sandhurst graduate who had been under virtual house arrest for seven years — the

△169

169. Enemy soldiers, when they first came warily into firqat encampments (probably after preliminary discussion via relatives at watering holes), were left by the SAS, unpressured and still armed, to talk to erstwhile comrades who had changed sides already. The existing firqat included brothers, cousins, uncles. Usually, within a few days, the converts — officially, Surrendered

Enemy Personnel, or 'SEP' — were ready to tell all they knew to SAS teams attached to the firqat or — as in this photograph — a British member of the Sultan's Intelligence Service.
170. Occasionally, the conversion was more dramatic. This was the only survivor of an 'adoo' (enemy) team encountered by the SAS on the jebel soon after the Battle of Mirbat. He eluded

mountainous southern province of Dhofar was a 'no-go' area for government forces. These forces were pressed into a narrow coastal strip, their backs to the sea, and it seemed only a matter of time before Dhofar and perhaps the whole of Oman was crushed by the same irresistible machine that had rolled over the Aden federation.

The SAS were introduced into Oman within days of Sultan Qaboos's coup d'état in July 1970. By then, with characteristic flair, the Regiment's leaders had already constructed a strategy for regaining the initiative and winning the war. The cornerstone of the plan, codenamed Operation 'Storm', was to change the style of government, and fighting, by offering liberalization instead of punishment to the enemy. It was a breath-taking, audacious plan to win

△170

capture but, a few days later, still armed with a Kalashnikov assault rifle, he descended to the small seaside town of Sudh to give himself up and join a pro-government firqat. The Soviet-made weapons of his dead comrades are laid out at his feet in this photograph, taken immediately after his surrender.

popular sympathy for the government, powerfully reinforced by emphasizing dedication to Islam, in contrast to the guerrillas' rejection of religion. Only for brief periods were more than one SAS squadron on the ground in Oman, a comparative handful of men. Before the war ended, there would be tens of thousands of men from Iran and Jordan in the field as well as the Sultan's own army. But as one SAS planner put it later, 'It wasn't our numbers but our ideas which counted' . . . The ideas, yes, and dedicated men of enormous endurance, patience and skill in making those ideas work. To turn round a righteously indignant and much abused population could not be achieved quickly. It was a slow, painstaking process of doing good in practical ways for a multitude of ordinary people, more like the accumulation of coral reef than the lightning conversion of Saul on the road to Tarsus. For the SAS it represented the ultimate expression of a diplomatic skill in handling primitive people which had started in Malaya, and which — as the Regiment's military environment changed — it would never be able to repeat.

Initially, the SAS felt its way cautiously into Oman, with just two four-man civil action teams, each with its medical centre staffed by the SAS, in the coastal towns of Mirbat and Taqa. Veterinary experts and even livestock were brought from Britain to create a model farm on the coastal plain near the provincial capital of Salalah.

Just as mastery of the jungle had been the key to the Malayan and Borneo campaigns, so in Dhofar it was the jebel — the mountain range straddling the province — wherein lay the obstacle and the opportunity to challenge the SAS philosophy. The turn of the tide began, if modestly, with an amnesty for guerrillas who surrendered. Some, who were unhappy about the brutality of the Communists in enforcing an end to both religious worship and tribal loyalty, decided they might be no worse off under the new régime of Qaboos. These men were then trained by the SAS and formed into a counter-guerrilla group known as a 'firqat'. They were trained, armed and paid but not directly commanded by the SAS. Firqats elected their leaders and every operation required complex negotiation and much persuasion. Orthodox soldiers in the Sultan's regular army thought it madness for British soldiers to go into the mountains to live with and be outnumbered by men who had recently been among the enemy. This was not irrational criticism. Some SAS soldiers achieved great rapport with the firqat and a few — such as Captain Simon Garthwaite — died trying to assist them under fire. Other SAS men found themselves in dangerously fragile situations when both firqat and SAS eyed one another with safety catches off. An SAS medic whose patient — a prominent firqat leader — died of a heart attack was in danger; so was the officer who refused his firqat instant leave, with a flight to the fleshpots thrown in. Every day, the average firqat presented a new psychological challenge to his British tutors. In a traditionally harsh society some firqat were genuine converts, but, for others, what mattered was to be on the winning side. Cupidity rather than idealism was their main

△171   △172   △173

motivation: the prospect of loot, whether it be new weapons, watering rights, women or cattle.

It was March 1971 before the first mixed force of about sixty firqat and forty SAS climbed an untried route to the mountains and marched along the plateau into territory untouched by regular forces for years. They stayed twelve days, fighting almost continuously a battle in which both sides used mortars and machine-guns as well as small arms. At least nine enemy were killed, and the number who took advantage of the amnesty rose significantly. Most important, the new firqat had shown itself resolute in battle. It was equally clear that if the hearts and minds of the jebel's indigenous population were to be won, then the Sultan's forces would have to be a permanent presence, but for this to be achieved, the supply of water, one way or another, was an absolute priority. In October, immediately after the monsoon, Operation 'Jaguar' established such a base at 'White City', inland near remote Jibjat. A week's hard fighting by several firqat groups, two SAS squadrons and 350 of the Sultan's regular army were needed for the job.

This was impressive, but even more so was the response of John Watts, the SAS colonel commanding the whole operation, to local pressures for normal trade to be resumed instantly. A total of 1,400 goats and several hundred head of cattle had to be transferred to market on the coast, or the firqat, whose tribal area this was in many cases, would fight no more. On 27 November, as Colonel Jeapes describes it, there was 'a Texan-style cattle drive supported by jet fighter cover and 5.5 inch artillery'. It was, he says, like something which blended a Boulting Brothers comedy with a John Wayne western. Other benefits — water wells, schools, government clinics and shops — would follow, with many of the enemy persuaded by their relatives in the firqats to change sides. It was not perfect; one firqat went on strike at a critical juncture during the military operation. But it was the prototype, a working model for ultimate victory, and astonishing progress in the eighteen months of SAS operations.

The following July the guerrillas made a brave, bold attempt to destroy the growing credibility of the government's new campaign. At dawn, under cover of low, monsoon cloud that would make it impossible for the Sultan's Air Force to intervene, 250 of the Communists' best fighting men, armed with medium machine-guns, automatic rifles, mortars, 75mm recoilless rifles and even an 84mm Carl Gustav rocket-launcher descended from the jebel and struck the coastal town of Mirbat, where the first SAS team had started work. The town was defended by 30 Askaris from northern Oman armed with bolt-action .303 rifles, a few firqatmen, 25 Dhofar Gendarmerie in a fort, armed with British-manufactured FN semi-automatic rifles, and an SAS training team. The latter consisted of nine men under the command of a young captain, Mike Kealy. On the flat roof of the team's house (known as the 'BATT house') were a heavy .5 Browning machine-gun and a lighter but powerful 'Jimpy' or general purpose machine-gun behind sandbags. The team also had an 81mm mortar.

The guerrillas swept across the defended hill north of the town, towards the fort. As exploding mortar bombs woke the team, two of the men manned the machine-guns and two more, both Fijian, raced 700 yards across open ground to join an Omani gunner on the garrison's only big weapon, a Second World War 25-pounder artillery gun. Two more manned the team's own mortar. The other two, including Kealy himself, used their rifles or ferried ammunition to the mortar and machine-gun teams, after sending a crisp radio message to headquarters, 40 miles away at Salalah, that they were under attack. For some time, the Fijian Corporal Labalaba had been firing and loading the 25-pounder single-handed, sighting at zero range down the barrel at the wire fence in front of the fort which the guerrillas were about to breach. Now came word that he was 'chinned, but all right'. Kealy, with a medical specialist, Trooper Tobin, darted through the smoke of battle to the gun pit. Their luck held. Tobin found the Omani gunner badly wounded, together with the second Fijian, who had propped himself up alongside the gun and was still firing his rifle. Labalaba was shot dead as he loaded the gun yet again, and Tobin was fatally wounded. The guerrillas closed on the pit, hurling grenades into it. Kealy and the second Fijian shot any who came too close, and Kealy snapped a radio message to the 'BATT house' requesting supporting fire from the machine-guns.

△174

△175

△176

By now, in spite of the low, 150ft cloud base, two Strike-master jets were hurtling towards the scene. They arrived in the nick of time, hitting the guerrillas with 500lb bombs and machine-gun fire. Back in Salalah, meanwhile, by the sort of coincidence that can turn defeat into victory, 23 men from a fresh SAS squadron were armed and ready to check their weapons on the range before taking over from Kealy's men. They flew to the scene in helicopters, landed on the edge of the town and attacked the guerrillas from the flank. The guerrillas, who had fought well in spite of their anticipation of an easy victory and symbolic occupation of Mirbat for a day, now cracked and withdrew.

It had been a very close shave. The enemy had come so close that the SAS mortarman had been obliged to remove the weapon from its bipod and hold it between his thighs to obtain sufficient elevation for the mortars to hit their target. The gun pit, and the area in front of it, resembled an abattoir. Kealy was awarded a DSO, Tobin a DCM, Labalaba a posthumous Mention in Despatches, and the corporal who had commanded the defence of the 'BATT house', a Military Medal. The battle had a disastrous effect on enemy morale, almost 100 of whom had been killed in action or subsequently died of their untreated wounds.

Over the next two years, Omani government forces added another potent technique to their armoury. These were a series of elaborate defensive lines running from the mountains to the coast. Manned at intervals, surrounded by mines, patrolled from the air as well as on the ground, they gradually throttled the guerrilla supply lines to their men still surviving in pockets of the jebel. The supplies came from South Yemen to the west of Oman. Not surprisingly, the nearer the Sultan's forces came to the border, the hotter the fighting became.

There was one particular enemy ordnance store that the SAS had wanted to get at for a long time. This was a vast collection of arms, ammunition and food in a complex series of caves at Sherishitti. The caves overlooked a wide wadi, or dried-up river bed. The Sultan's forces — elements of his regular army stiffened by the presence of SAS soldiers and firqat irregulars — had to fight hard through dense under-growth, against a determined enemy, even to get within

171-176. The quality of fighting men within any given firqat varied from excellent to Gilbertian. A group of SEPs came as a job lot and they were often related. There was no question of the SAS screening out individuals, so the soldiers in the Firqat al-A'asifat ranged from this one-eyed boy armed with an old Lee Enfield .303 rifle (**171**) to the hard man carrying the Soviet 7.62mm SKS carbine (**172**); from the greybeard with his spotless FN 7.62mm Nato FAL rifle (**173**) to a canny veteran resembling Fagin (**174**); from men in their prime (**175**) to a youngster armed with an apparently well used SAS M16 Armalite (**176**). The M16 has many plastic parts, making it conveniently light. The spike attached to the barrel was used to dislodge cartridges stuck in the breech; in action, jams of that sort were embarrassing. While the boy poses, an older comrade, unmoved by the camera, carries on making bread.

marching distance of the wadi. On the second day, a British officer commanding a company of the Sultan's forces, rejecting the advice of a veteran SAS corporal, decided to advance across open ground down the forward slope of one side of the wadi. When a substantial part of his company had abandoned cover, a devastating barrage of enemy fire opened up on them from the other side of the valley. The company lost 13 dead and 22 wounded in less than an hour. For the rest of that day, the SAS fought a savage battle to restore the morale of their allies, hitting back with machine-gun and mortar fire to provide cover for the survivors running back to shelter. One wounded man was carried out by an SAS Fijian soldier after three of the Sultan's regulars had dropped him in their haste to reach safety. Another casualty was wounded again as he was being treated by an SAS medic. The caves were not occupied by government forces until the war ended more than a year later, but the enemy were denied their use, also. From high ground taken during the preliminary battle, Saladin armoured cars kept the area under continuous fire.

The decisive last battle, in October 1975, surprised even its principal British architect, Brigadier John Akehurst. Since 1972, his forces had established a vast hilltop position at Sarfait, near the border with South Yemen. It was per-petually surrounded by enemy soldiers, including some regulars from South Yemen, and could be resupplied only by air; and even this, in view of the surface-to-air missiles used by the other side, was hazardous. Akehurst planned an elaborate assault, using helicopters as troop transports to establish yet another defensive barrier across the mountains and down to the coast. Meanwhile, Omani troops were to divert enemy attention by 'breaking out' of the Sarfait position down steps cut in the rock. These diversionary troops, led by Lieutenant-Colonel Ian Christie of the Muscat Regiment, were astonished to encounter virtually no opposition as they probed onward. Christie consolidated the ground he had taken with more troops. Akehurst discarded months of careful planning by pouring more troops into the newly occupied ground. South Yemen responded by shelling the positions, only to be countered by Sultan Qaboos who hit back at the Yemeni guns in Hauf with air strikes. A peace agreement, negotiated by neutral Arab governments, was signed a few months later in March 1976.

The Dhofar campaign was unique in that British soldiers systematically fought alongside recently Surrendered Enemy Personnel. In addition, unlike other SAS campaigns after the Second World War, it was fought against an enemy equipped with artillery and Katyusha missiles the size of telegraph poles, as well as Kalashnikov AK47 assault

△177

177-179. An early British experiment to emulate the Communists by mingling different tribes in one firqat broke down under the impact of inter-tribal rivalries and jealousy, so most firqat units were tribally based, fighting on their own territory. The men of Firqat al-A'asifat, members of the Mahra tribe, were a temperamental lot. Initially, they had walked many miles out of the mountains to make contact with the SAS at a fly-blown spot on the edge of the Empty Quarter known as Barbezum. (Photograph

177 shows the area's characteristic desolation.) Sometimes they launched operations against the enemy without support from the SAS or anyone else. Occasionally, they would go on strike while playing a key role in larger combined operations. Before going into action (and sometimes after) the firqat would debate the matter in 'wigwam' parliaments (**178**). Here (**179**), members of Firqat al-A'asifat are seen stripping a dead camel of meat to be dried in the sun and carried on operations.

180-182. Attempts to supply Barbezum

by lorry usually ended with the vehicle being blown up by mines (**180**). Although many mines were cleared by the SAS and the firqat (**181**), it was usually necessary to fly supplies to Barbezum and elsewhere by Skyvan (**182**). With its short take-off capability and rugged landing gear, the aircraft was ideal for the job. Its appearance heralded for SAS soldiers 'the weekly fresh' — properly cooked, wholesome food with enough vitamins to stave off scurvy — and mail from home, as well as urgent medical supplies.

rifles. (At Sarfait, one SAS troop was reputed to have come under heavier fire than anything experienced by British soldiers since the Korean War in the 1950s.) The first of these factors made it critically important for the SAS to motivate former enemies to fight and remain loyal. Equally important, because of the firepower available to the enemy, was the ability to build quickly rock shelters, known as 'sangars'' before incoming mortar bombs, shells and missiles landed. Both elements — firqat problems and enemy firepower — combined with climate and terrain to make Dhofar one of the hardest campaigns ever fought by the Regiment. Only the SAS could have delivered what was

required: professional soldiering plus enough patient, social psychology to win the war of perceptions.

Two months before the peace treaty ending the Dhofar conflict, in January 1976, the SAS was publicly committed by Prime Minister Harold Wilson, in an inspired but embarrassing publicity stroke, to troubles nearer home, in Northern Ireland. The effect of that unexpected statement was at least as disconcerting as the Regiment's sudden move from Malaya, after almost ten years, to Northern Oman. Militarily, as well as politically, it was another world.

△178   ▽179   ▽180

▽181   ▽182

183-187. Weapons training by Arabic speaking SAS soldiers was a form of communication that broke down cultural barriers in a community dedicated to arms. Live grenade practice with the firqat sometimes had to be approached with caution. Some people picked up the art quickly and with confidence (**183**); some were more diffident (**184**); and others just did not get the hang of it at all (**185**). Here (**186**), an instructor gives his firqat pupil tuition in the use of an initiation device for a Claymore mine. Firqat veterans, some of them trained in guerrilla warfare in Russia and China as well as South Yemen, were already highly competent, such as this group (**187**) firing a versatile Chinese 60mm mortar. The SAS could still teach them new tricks of the trade, such as applying a squirt of petrol down the barrel to increase the weapon's range.

188-190. At the beginning of SAS intervention in the war in 1970, the Sultan's regular forces were suffering from 'jebelitis', or a reluctance to stay in the mountains (and be shot at continuously) for more than a day. Here (**188**), an SAS patrol in those early days sets off to test enemy reaction. When the men neared base on their return, it was noticeable that they relaxed, closing the gap between them (**189**). The machine-gunner (**190**), labouring past a defensive sangar, is carrying a 'jimpy' (general-purpose machine-gun, capable of splitting a rock to kill an enemy hiding behind it). This particular gun was already mounted on its tripod, adding to the soldier's formidable load of back-pack and ammunition.

△**183**

▽**188**

△184 △185 △186 △187 ▽189 ▽190

191-195. After the first permanent SAS stronghold was established on the jebel, the guerrillas hit back in July 1972 at Mirbat, a seaside town occupied by ten SAS soldiers. In the epic battle that followed, six of the SAS team replied with machine-guns and a mortar from their BATT (for 'British Army Training Team') house (**191, 192**). The machine-guns, a .5 Browning and a GPMG, were behind sandbags on the roof, with the mortar on the ground immediately below. The mortar was an 81mm like this one (**193**) being fired in an orthodox way by two SAS soldiers in Dhofar. But, at Mirbat, so close were the enemy that one of the defenders had to elevate the weapon higher than the bipod permitted; he held it between his thighs to lift the trajectory. Under cover of darkness and low, monsoon cloud, the guerrillas descended from mountains overlooking the position. They then cut off Mirbat. The defenders had their backs to the sea; there was no escape. The guerrillas' main target was an isolated fort in front of the town occupied by the Dhofar Gendarmerie. And it was over the 700-yard space, seen here from the 'BATT house' (**194**), that the young SAS officer Mike Kealy, as well as Trooper Tobin, the Fijian SAS Corporal Labalaba and another Fijian still serving with the Regiment, crossed to defend the fort. The area was swept by intensive fire as, loaded with ammunition and emergency medical supplies, they ran, dodged and ducked their way to their objective. Only one of the four is still alive. After the battle, one of the survivors awaits evacuation to hospital (**195**).

196-199. The farther the SAS penetrated into the mountains the greater was the resistance they and their allies encountered. Sangars became deeper, more elaborate (**196**). A favourite weapon was the old but effective .5 Browning (**197**), some of which had to be retrieved from military museums in Britain and brought back into service. As the war stepped up, artillery controlled by the SAS included this 25-pounder of Second World War vintage, seen here (**198**) in action at 'White City', the first permanent mountain base established by the SAS. But even this was no match for the modern, Soviet-made 122mm Katyusha, a missile from which exploded 100 yards ahead of the sangar as this picture (**199**) was taken. A direct hit by such a missile on one SAS sangar cut in half the soldier sheltering behind it.

200. Another memorable action was fought on Jebel Aram in May 1971. The objective was a 75mm artillery gun which, hidden among rocks and bushes on the mountain, was shelling the seaside town of Taqa, where an SAS firqat training team was established. Conditions in Taqa were as irksome, in some ways, as on the jebel itself. Here, SAS soldiers queue for food in the confined, reinforced kitchen of their 'BATT house'. They were destined to take part in an intense three-day gun battle, which inflicted heavy casualties on the guerrillas and led to the destruction of valuable emergency food supplies, but did not capture the gun.

201-202. Living conditions at Mirbat, by comparison with Taqa, were slightly less cramped. On its return, this patrol (**201**) wasted no time in settling down to dinner. It was taken Arab-style, communally (**202**).

△196

▽199   △200

△197

△198

△201

△202

203, 204. One of the toughest mountain outposts, near the big guerrilla ordnance store of Sherishitti, was known as 'the position at Defa'. It was from Defa that the ill-fated Sherishitti expedition was launched in January 1975. And it was from Defa (**203**), in September the same year, that a patrol led by the SAS went looking for an enemy Katyusha. A confused, close-quarter battle among bushes in morning mist followed, in which Lance Corporal Geordie Small sustained a bullet wound from which he bled to death. Other SAS casualties included Lance Corporal Tony Fleming (formerly an Army Physical Training Corps sergeant-major), who was hit by a bullet that severed his spinal column. A third SAS soldier, hit by a series of bullets including one which passed through his neck, survived, recovered and is still serving with the Regiment. This picture (**204**) of spent mortar cases is a vivid illustration of the intensity of the conflict there. At one stage, 2,000 rounds were fired from the position in a week.

205, 206. Surprisingly in such a setting, the most important weapons were those of economics and psychology. The government's provision of water wells, with drilling equipment ordered by the SAS and brought specially from Britain, was a seductive currency in the parched mountains. The cultivation of religion — denied by the Communists — was just as important to many devout Muslims. Here (**205**), firqat warriors face Mecca and pray on a windy battlefield. Treatment by SAS medics was welcomed by people of all ages and — rare in the world of Islam — by both sexes (**206**).

207, 208. Throughout the war, the SAS clinics remained active and busy, receiving some unexpected social as well as medical problems. At this one at Mirbat (**207**), the patient was a young woman, brought to the clinic by her mother (**208**). The girl was suffering from a stomach ailment. When the medical staff asked whether she had missed a period, her mother replied 'She has not been with any man'. It was clear to one of the more experienced SAS 'bush doctors' that the girl was pregnant (as she was later proved to be). He reacted by walking to the window, opening it and looking out for a long time. His companion asked, 'Why are you looking out of the window?' 'Well,' came the reply, 'it's a long time since anything like this happened. In fact, the last time, three wise men came from the East, following a star . . .'

209. Enemy deaths, the SAS men were reminded, were to be treated as a matter for regret rather than rejoicing. Casualties such as these could well be brothers of those fighting alongside the British. In reality, as in any civil war, enemy deaths — irrespective of race — were not unwelcome to those on the other side.

210. In the world of Islam, the end of Ramadan, the period of fasting during the daylight hours, ends with the greatest of Muslim feasts known as The Feast, or 'Id. In spite of official dispensations from the fast — dispensations that were not always observed — the war in Dhofar almost stopped for 'Id, particularly at Mirbat where this photograph was taken. There was much dancing and chanting outside the Dhofar Gendarmerie fort, marching and beating of drums; salutes for the SAS and, to the chagrin of the British soldiers, gleeful expenditure of expensive ammunition into the air.

△203

△206

△204

△205

▽209

△207

△208 ▽210

◁211　　　△212　△213　▽214

▽215

211-215. The final phase of operations, in the autumn of 1975, was launched from the hill position of Sarfait, between Defa and the border with South Yemen. It was intended as a diversion to fool the enemy, but it encountered remarkably little opposition and became the main axis of advance from the mountain to the coast, finally closing the door on guerrilla supplies from South Yemen. In part at least, this unexpected success was because the Defa operations, farther east, had drawn in so many of the guerrilla reserves. The 'push after Defa' did not achieve the breakthrough the planners had intended. Instead, it acted as a fatal lure for the enemy, sapping his strength. At close quarters, SAS soldiers, like this man from 'A' Squadron (**211**), used grenades. Here (**212**) the mortars are prepared for action from shallow, lightly sandbagged pits. The firqat (**213**) are armed with a Soviet RPG-7 rocket-propelled grenade launcher. The Regiment's snipers gave the enemy no respite by day (**214**); but, by night, firqat ambushes were put in position to catch the opposition at dawn. The immediate objective was usually to conquer the high ground, establish a sangar and — when there was time — to sleep alongside it (**215**). Soon, these men would move on to another country, another campaign. They left Oman in better shape than they had found it.

Contemporary conflict
The dirty war

While most SAS soldiers were engaged in the gladiatorial combat in Oman, an entirely different form of warfare was evolving in the cities of Europe and the United States. It was a war in which random victims, many of them children, were kidnapped, mutilated and murdered in the name of idealism. Urban terrorism in itself is not a new phenomenon. During the Roman occupation of Palestine, Jewish zealots formed terrorist groups to assassinate collaborators. The mechanism of terrorism then was the same as it is today: psychological intimidation.

Two factors have made this form of psychological warfare uniquely powerful since the mid-sixties. First, the evolution of satellite television meant that events could be transmitted, as they happened, to homes in any part of the world. Second, the use of terrorism by governments as a cost-effective form of warfare — war by proxy — meant that some terrorist groups had at their disposal funds and training facilities sometimes superior to those of the security forces they would oppose. In an age when the use of orthodox armies to project foreign policy could trigger off the nuclear armoury, the constraint of nuclear destruction was another incentive for states to use irregular 'freedom fighters' instead.

The massacre of eleven Israeli athletes at the Munich Olympics in 1972 illustrates both factors. The worldwide television audience watching that affair was estimated to be 500 million people and — as Richard Clutterbuck argues — if only a tiny percentage had sympathy for the terrorists' cause, 'a tiny percentage of 500 million is still a lot of people'. Another authority, Walter Laqueur, cites reports that the 'Black September' organization, which engineered the Munich massacre, received a seven million dollar budget for the job. For public consumption, however, terrorist groups of every political persuasion still try — and among the young and gullible, succeed — in claiming that their form of violence is ideologically pure because it is 'the weapon of the weak against the strong'.

The SAS had been interested in counter-terrorism — known as 'Counter Revolutionary Warfare' to avoid overtones of the term counter-terror — for some years before Munich, though that event marked a turning point in government thinking about the problem. Urban Aden had been the main target of the Marxists' 'liberation' campaign in the mid-sixties. One of the Arab leaders there, Abdul Fatah Ismail, believed that the struggle in the countryside was not worthwhile because no attention would be paid to it abroad. Faced with a skilful campaign of selective assassination of intelligence officers, as well as the less discriminate use of hand grenades to attack British schoolchildren, the SAS evolved in urban Aden undercover 'keeni-meeni' squads dressed as Arabs to trawl the most likely target areas and ambush the terrorists.

Few people yet believed that such tactics would be necessary in Britain. An experiment by men of 21 SAS to deal with a hypothetical terrorist attack on London's Underground system did not get off the drawing board because it was politically sensitive, and unnecessary. In fact, the threat was closer to home than most people realized. The Aden withdrawal occurred in 1967. Paris erupted in left-wing student riots in the summer of 1968 and, in Northern Ireland, agitation for legitimate civil rights was already provoking street violence. At Hereford, meanwhile, men of 22 SAS were acquiring, or polishing, recently acquired techniques of marksmanship suitable for the confined circumstances of this sort of warfare. In part, this was because of the use of the Regiment after Aden as bodyguards, and bodyguard trainers, in various parts of the world. The Close Quarter Battle (CQB) House, colloquially known as 'the Killing House', provided unique experience in the delicate work of drawing a concealed weapon and disabling the 'bad guy' without accidentally killing the VIP who was being protected.

With the start of the Dhofar campaign in 1970, this sort of training became a side issue. Back at Hereford, a modest counter-revolutionary wing remained in being as a means of keeping in touch with what was happening, but it would be some time before the Regiment was actively involved in combating a political virus that was spreading through the Americas and the Middle East as well as Europe. This did not mean that the Regiment's thinkers were blind to the mounting risks to internal security in the United Kingdom, as they perceived them at the time. Early in 1972, a discussion paper on the subject was submitted to the Director of Military Operations at the Defence Ministry.

As it happened, the first international terrorist threat proved to be a damp squib, an elaborate false alarm. In May 1972, an anonymous telephone call to the New York offices of Cunard, owners of the liner *Queen Elizabeth 2*, announced that six bombs planted on board the vessel would explode and sink her unless a ransom of £134,000 were paid. The ship was then 1,000 miles from Britain with 1,438 passengers on board. Sergeant Clifford Oliver of 22 SAS joined a mixed team of Royal Marine SBS commandos and an explosives expert in a parachute drop into the Atlantic near the liner. At the time, the Regiment was already studying various hijack scenarios including, for example, the seizure of a supertanker at sea. No bombs were found aboard *QE 2* and the soldiers enjoyed a socially eventful trip back to Britain.

A few months later, the prolonged agony of the Israeli Olympic athletes began at Munich on a stage already attended by the world's radio and television news teams. With two athletes already murdered, the 'Black September' team of seven took nine more Israelis with them to Fürstenfeldbruck airport with a promise of safe conduct to Egypt. At the airport, German police marksmen made a disastrous attempt to kill or disable the terrorists, resulting in the deaths of all the surviving hostages and five terrorists. The surviving terrorists, although captured, were later released under pressure of yet another hijack. (This pattern was to be repeated elsewhere.) Munich starkly demonstrated the extent to which democratic government now faced a 'no-win' situation. The alternatives, it seemed, were surrender to blackmail or overkill which would expose

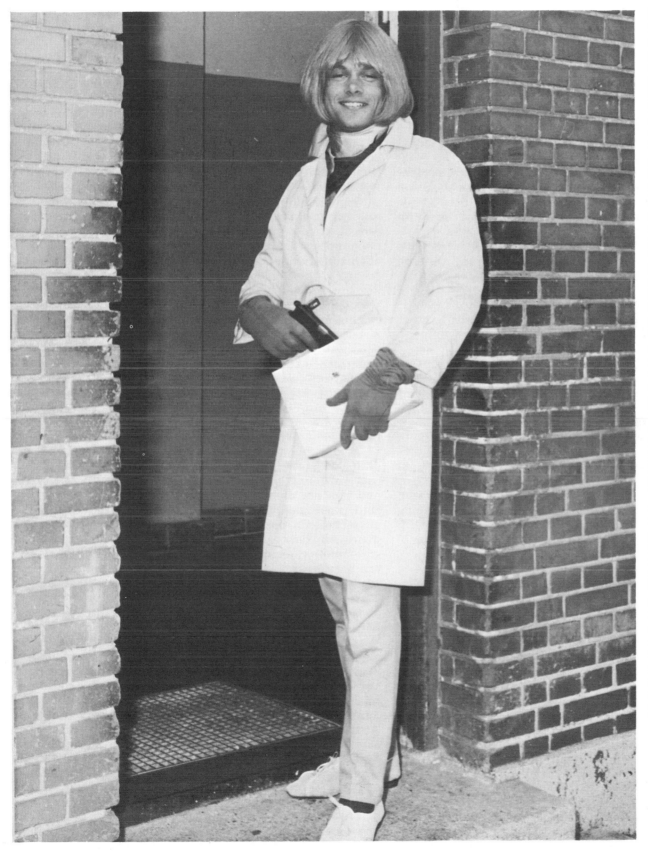

216. Unconventional warfare — and most contemporary armed conflict is in that category — requires ingenuity, lack of inhibition and, occasionally, a convincing disguise. This bold experiment by a trooper in 21 SAS did not quite succeed because the disguise was not sufficiently contemporary. The unit was taking part in a test of security at a Danish naval base in 1971. The trooper concerned almost talked his way past the guard until someone noticed that he was wearing slacks at a time when 'hot pants' were in vogue. Two SAS soldiers who penetrated the German front line in France during the Second World War were more successful in their use of the same gambit, but they dressed as unfashionable peasant women. The 1971 exercise started with a para-drop that caused seventeen casualties, five of them stretcher cases. Two men, entangled in the air, landed on one parachute.

elected government (though not the terrorists) to popular accusations of mismanagement and brutality.

The West German Government reacted by creating a special anti-terrorist unit known as GSG-9. In London, Prime Minister Edward Heath inquired about Defence Ministry contingency plans to deal with a similar threat. This demand provoked some embarrassment in Whitehall, as did a similar one some years later from Prime Minister Callaghan, in the wake of a rescue of French hostages in Zaire by Foreign Legion paratroopers. Military men hate to concede that there is any contingency, however remote, which they have not at least considered. After a hasty search through the files, the SAS document was produced with the explanation that it had not yet been processed. Heath studied the documents and within hours ordered that the SAS CRW wing be developed with all speed and whatever budget was required. From then on it received sophisticated equipment, including electronic devices; greater mobility; new weapons more suited for use in a confined space; and more manpower.

The Regiment's own operational research department devised a weapon intended to blind and stun the opposition during the first vital seconds of a siege-busting attack. Exercises were mounted against a variety of potential targets ranging from office blocks to railway trains. Local police forces participated in these, to evaluate not only SAS effectiveness but also to calculate whether — if this were the

217. During the period that ended with the withdrawal from Aden in 1967 and the beginning of the Dhofar campaign in 1970, the SAS was not, for once, engaged in warfare requiring the attention of a full squadron, serving on rota in a combat capacity. In part, those years were occupied with VIP protection, with teams occasionally acting as bodyguards for heads of state useful to Britain; more frequently, training the bodyguards of the state requesting such assistance. A good professional bodyguard is a rare animal. He has to be alert, intelligent and able to blend into the social scenery on state occasions. He must also be an expert driver, capable of eluding a street ambush by driving through a barrier or making a vertiginously fast three-point turn. Even more important, he must be capable of over-ruling the potentate he is guarding, if this is a matter of life or death. When the tricks of escape and evasion do not work, he must be capable of shooting back calmly and accurately. In 1981, an SAS officer driving alone in Bogside, Londonderry, was ambushed by a car containing four Provisional IRA men who started shooting at him. He stopped, took cover in the street behind the open door of his car, and then picked off his assailants. Two were killed and a third was seriously injured. The fourth, a driver, fled with the injured man. A potential bodyguard unit in an African state is seen here practising under the watchful eye of its SAS instructor.

real thing — the soldiers could be accused of using excessive force to achieve their objective. In such a situation it is not inconceivable that the police force to which the SAS gave its assistance might be obliged to arrest and prosecute the soldiers whose aid they had invoked. (Such an event did occur in Northern Ireland.) The paradox is a necessary one. In spite of left-wing mythology, the SAS soldier has no 'licence to kill': unlike the terrorist, he is subject to the rule of law in Britain rather than the law of the jungle. As subsequent events would prove, these were wise precautions.

Given this background, the SAS was less concerned during the years between 1972 and 1976 with the nationalist/sectarian terror of Ireland than with the Dhofar campaign and the threat of terrorism in Britain. This, to be sure, included IRA terror, but equally the activities of middle class chic revolutionaries such as the Baader-Meinhoff group and its allies within the lunatic left, and the various Palestinian gangs with which they were also linked. As terror became internationally organized — and such organization had started with a conference in Havana in 1966 — so did the response of democratic governments. The SAS concluded, correctly, that assassination, as such, was a weapon of limited utility to any group wishing to put pressure on government over a substantial period of time. Such an outrage happens, shocks, and fades into obscurity too rapidly, but the kidnap of a public figure, with regular bulletins from or about him, can hold the headlines much longer, as can a well organized hijack and siege. The hijack of an aircraft creates a travelling publicity circus for terrorism, and the potency of the formula is even stronger (but only in a democratic society) if such methods are used during a general election or a US presidential year.

For all these reasons, the SAS teams rehearsed not only siege-breaking tactics, as at Heathrow, Gatwick and Stansted airports in 1974 and 1975, but also sent small teams to cooperate in major anti-terrorist operations in Italy and Holland. Their discreet presence was aimed at studying the victories and errors of both sides in this new style of warfare, as well as to give practical help to Britain's allies. Only rarely did these activities become public knowledge. In December 1975, a Provisional IRA team, trapped in a flat at Balcombe Street, Marylebone, with a middle-aged couple living there as hostages, surrendered to the London police when the BBC announced that the SAS was on the scene, ready to attack. This was a victory for SAS mystique. In May/June 1977, SAS advisers were present during the double siege mounted by Moluccan terrorists on a commuter train in Assen, Holland and at the nearby village school of Bovensmilde. Their offer of stun grenades was declined, but the Dutch did use similar methods in throwing the terrorists into confusion at the moment of assault. In October 1977, Major Alastair Morrison, OBE, MC and Sergeant Barry Davies, BEM, a pair of SAS veterans, joined with West Germany's GSG-9 team in an assault on a Lufthansa airliner to free 87 hostages in Mogadishu. This time the Regiment's stun grenades were used, and after a confused gun battle inside the aircraft the hostages were liberated. When Aldo Moro, president of Italy's Christian Democratic Party, was ambushed and kidnapped in a battle in which his five bodyguards were gunned down in 1978, the SAS played an active role in organizing a new anti-terrorist squad in Italy. This did not save Moro, who was shot eleven times by his Red Brigades captors.

By now, the Regiment was also acquiring knowledge of such events from the experience of officers who had completed their service with the Regiment to work for private organizations, such as Control Risks, in managing kidnap risks among businessmen. In some cases this required negotiation with the kidnappers. According to Richard Clutterbuck, 'In their first 50 cases Control Risks advised negotiators facing total demands amounting to over 300 million dollars. About 60 million in all was paid in ransoms and all but three of the victims live to tell the tale.'

By the time a group of semi-literate dockers from a part of Iran claimed by Iraq as 'Arabistan' came to London to seize the Iranian Embassy in 1980, the SAS had a finely tuned machine to deal with just such an eventuality. For seven years it had repeatedly rehearsed management of the crisis, including relations with the police who would handle negotiations with the terrorists. The SAS exercise scenario reflected the belief that it should go into action only after prolonged negotiations and terrorist threats had culminated in the murder of a hostage, an event that would be signalled by the depositing of the victim's corpse on the doorstep of the seized building. In the event, the embassy operation, codenamed 'Nimrod', followed the pattern.

Two SAS teams from the same squadron were involved in the attack. The first was a perimeter group of marksmen with sniper rifles, who ringed the building. The second team stormed into it behind explosive charges planted against the embassy's bullet-proof windows after a stealthy approach across balconies and — at the back of the building — down abseil ropes from the roof. During the assault, CS riot-gas canisters set alight the front curtains and the fire rapidly spread. One SAS soldier, trapped on a faulty rope, found himself being 'spit roasted' as his weight swung him inward. During the first, critical seconds, a terrorist turned his gun on hostages huddled in the centre of the embassy's second floor telex room, murdering one man and wounding two others. Seconds later, when two SAS soldiers burst into the room, the gunmen claimed, in Farsi, that they were surrendering. They were shot dead; until then they had shown no inclination to give up their weapons or hostages. They had claimed that the building would be destroyed by an explosive charge if this sort of assault came in, and the SAS team's first priority was to take any steps necessary to get the hostages out alive. In the event, one terrorist armed with a grenade did try to leave the building among the hostages but was shot. Another, who succeeded in merging with his former captives, was arrested in the embassy garden. Meanwhile, the team that entered from the back of the building included the man trapped on his abseil rope, which had been unceremoniously cut to drop him a considerable distance. One of the same group smashed through a rear window to discover the terrorist leader, Awn Ali Mohammed ('Salim') about to shoot him. Police Constable Trevor Lock, a hostage who had concealed his .38 revolver throughout the five-day ordeal, grappled with him until Awn, too, was shot dead by the SAS.

The circumstances in which the siege ended — safe release of those hostages not murdered by the terrorists; the death or capture of the terrorists themselves by the SAS — was magnified by live television coverage in a way that turned the propaganda of the deed against the terrorist cause. But still there were people in the British media dedicated to belief in an SAS 'licence to kill' outside the law. After the inquest on the terrorists, and the verdict of lawful homicide, a BBC television programme asked, 'What if the verdict had been different?' and proceeded to discuss events as if this were the case. It was an extraordinary display of journalistic dogma.

As it happened, and it happened tragically, the truth had been demonstrated in another siege, in Belfast, only a few days before the Iranian Embassy affair was concluded. In Ireland, an SAS team led by Captain Richard Westmacott attacked a house occupied by an IRA group armed with an M60 general purpose machine-gun. This was used to kill Westmacott, after which sheets were displayed in a clear signal of surrender. Eight IRA men were taken into custody, unharmed and handed over to the police. Subsequently, they all escaped from Crumlin Road Prison, Belfast. Four were convicted in their absence of Westmacott's murder and were still at large almost a year later. Unlike the SAS, they do claim a 'licence to kill' their political opponents.

The involvement of the Regiment in the Irish troubles has its origins in the wave of violence that scorched Belfast and Londonderry in 1969. What had started, for the British Army as a whole, as an emergency peace-keeping job to protect Catholic ghettoes in 1969 had been turned round by the manipulators of a civil rights campaign into the ancient feud against British occupation of Ireland. Both were steps on a road towards demolishing the elected government in Dublin and the creation of an Irish 'workers' republic'. The terror was always double edged, for the Protestant community was equally efficient in the hideous trade of intimidation, murder and arson as instruments of local politics. During those early, traumatic days of 1969, 'D' Squadron of the SAS was sent to Northern Ireland to stop potential gun runners. With earlier history in mind, the British Government was as much concerned with Protestant as Catholic weapons, so 'D' Squadron patrolled the glens and coast of Antrim, and drew a blank. Regimentally, the tour was memorable only for a commemorative parade to the Newtonards grave of the late Colonel Paddy Mayne. A few months later, Operation 'Storm' began in Dhofar and that was that.

And yet, in June 1973, the Northern Ireland Civil Rights Association published a bulletin headlined, 'What To Do If The SAS Shoot You'. There were many unsolved sectarian murders at the time. Subsequently, a careful analysis of these by journalists Martin Dillon and Denis Lehane concluded: 'Many Catholics believe . . . that the British Army has been responsible for the bulk of the killings . . . Our investigations contradict this. Only two deaths out of 200 examined can categorically be laid at the door of the Army. Of the handful of eight killings which we have been unable to attribute, none seems likely to have been committed by the Army. Nor are there statistically very many cases of attempted assassinations where Army involvement is inconclusive.'

The confusion about the role of the SAS in Ireland at that time appears to derive from the presence of other plain clothes Army patrols operating as a Military Reconnaissance Force (MRF). These, almost certainly, were the brainchild of another counter-insurgency veteran, Brigadier (later General) Sir Frank Kitson. As an entirely different entity, SAS teams did carry out covert surveillance work from time to time in the province, solely to obtain information. Some of its officers were also in key positions in the world of military intelligence at a time when conflicting agencies appeared to be operating as much against one another as against the terrorists. The agents whose work the SAS controlled included, for instance, Captain Robert Nairac, who was murdered by the IRA in 1977. Such agents were not SAS soldiers. The relationship between them and the Regiment was an elevated version of that between the SAS and the firqat in Dhofar, with the difference that before 1976 the SAS was not committed to a combat role.

The only exception to these limited commitments by the Regiment prior to 1976 — involving a handful of people —

was a brief period during 1974. Captured IRA documents had convinced the British Prime Minister, Harold Wilson, that the terrorist organization was about to trigger off a full-scale sectarian civil war with attacks on Protestant areas. The documents were genuine, but open to two interpretations. The correct one was that the scheme was a last ditch, 'doomsday' contingency plan to be used if a pogrom against Catholic areas were launched. But, in the panic that followed the plan's discovery, much of one SAS squadron was drafted into Northern Ireland to augment the intelligence-gathering activities of the MRF, Royal Ulster Constabulary Special Branch, MI5, MI6, and the Special Branch of the police south of the border, the Gardai. This hiccup apart, SAS involvement in Northern Ireland, as in Dhofar, grew slowly and cautiously after a late start.

When, finally, the Regiment was publicly and formally committed to Ulster, squadron by squadron as in Oman, it was taken by surprise. The Wilson announcement moved Colonel David Stirling, the Regiment's founder, to remark, 'Not really stealthy, was it, the way they put the SAS in Northern Ireland?' Wilson's announcement, to placate Protestant opinion outraged by the murder of ten unarmed Protestants taken from a bus near the border, was made at a time when only a dozen SAS soldiers were instantly available. In the event, the mystique that the Irish attached

to the SAS, and the belief in their own propaganda about the Regiment, were the most valuable assets it had had for some time.

The warfare to which the Regiment was first sent, on the unmarked border in rolling, wooded country, was a classic guerrilla conflict where he who shoots first, and most accurately, survives. Such confrontations invariably left the IRA badly mauled by seasoned veterans of the Dhofar jebel, and the border area became unusually calm for many months after the SAS arrived. But, in general, Ireland bore a closer resemblance to the battle for media attention and sympathy on the international terrorist scene than the gladiatorial combat of Oman. The IRA and its sympathizers, although they did not recognize judicial institutions on either side of the border, were ready enough to use the judicial process when it seemed to offer a propaganda point or two. The SAS learned such lessons the hard way.

Two patrols which entered the Irish Republic and then pleaded that they had misread maps on the ill-defined border were prosecuted before a court in Dublin. Subsequently, when an SAS team staked out on an IRA weapons store shot the 16-year-old youth who drew a weapon from it, two men from the team were tried for murder. As prosecuting counsel put it, 'The security forces do not have a free hand to . . . claim the same immunity as if they were on the

battlefield.' The soldiers were acquitted, but the affair underlined the unique constraints under which they had to fight; constraints that ultimately added up to Westmacott's death and freedom for the men who murdered him.

In common with the rest of the security forces, the SAS now faced an awkward dilemma. The use of excessive force by the Parachute Regiment and the deaths of people not involved in the conflict were the ingredients of 'Bloody Sunday' in Londonderry in 1972. Such an event can raise sympathy and funds for terrorists well beyond the United States. At the other extreme, the killing of eighteen soldiers of the Parachute Regiment on the border near Warrenpoint several years later, in a series of neatly executed land mine and machine-gun attacks, was a straight military defeat. As such, it was also a public relations catastrophe internationally.

Asked which sort of problem he would prefer to live with in Ireland, one thoughtful SAS officer with extensive Irish experience commented: 'If I had to choose between another 'Bloody Sunday' and another Warrenpoint, I would choose Warrenpoint.' Not all of his comrades would agree, but the comment encapsulates the Regiment's problem of defeating terrorism in a modern environment. It also says everything about the attitude of the SAS to its mythical 'licence to kill'. It does not have such a licence — and it does not seek one.

△219

◁218   △220

218. In 1972, an SAS sergeant participated in one of the first tests of Britain's capacity to respond to terrorist threats; in this case, a claim that six bombs had been planted on board the Cunard liner *QE 2*. With men of the Royal Marine SBS, he was parachuted into the Atlantic, 1,000 miles from Britain, to deal with the threat. The call was a hoax, but resulted in useful experience in inter-service cooperation. The RAF supplied the Hercules aircraft from which the drop was made, and a Nimrod maritime reconnaissance aircraft to provide instant and secure radio communications between the team and its British base.
219. By 1972 and 1973, it was clear that

the main target of the international terrorist was the world's civil air fleet. The advantage of an aerial hijack was that it was a mobile vehicle for propaganda, attracting publicity at each refuelling stop. The SAS was given the main task of handling such sieges, for example at Stansted, when peaceful methods of negotiation had failed. Larger, more elaborate exercises at Heathrow and Gatwick airports in 1974 and 1975 also involved more orthodox units equipped with Scorpion light tanks, and armoured cars. During one of these exercises, this Life Guards soldier manned a Nato 7.62mm Bren Gun on the Heathrow perimeter track, while SAS men were

mingling more discreetly with civilians in the departure lounge.
220. Balcombe Street, Marylebone, London, December 1975: Four IRA gunmen are cornered by armed police in a flat owned by a middle-aged couple who are now hostages. The couple were leading their lives, harming no-one, when the gunmen burst into their home. Now an SAS team is on stand-by, ready to assault the building if this becomes necessary. After five exhausting days, the increasingly irrational terrorists learn from a BBC radio news bulletin the strength of the opposition, and surrender.

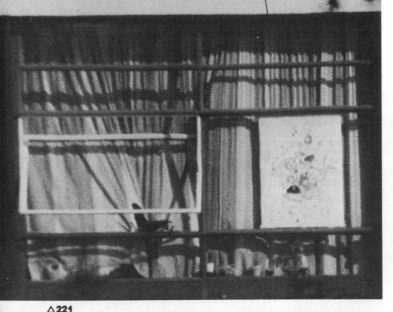

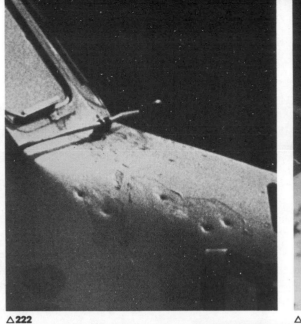

△221
△222
△223

△224
△225

221, 222. By 1977 — nine years after the onset of political violence in Paris and Northern Ireland — there was increasing cooperation among western European governments to combat terrorism of all kinds. In a pioneering effort that year, teams from both the West German GSG-9 organization and the SAS flew to Holland to assist the Dutch Government. Young Asians of Moluccan extraction, born and educated in Holland, seized a village school containing 105 children at Bovensmilde and a commuter train at Assen. The terrorists were in pursuit of an impossible demand: that Indonesia (a former Dutch colony) hand over part of its territory to the non-existent state of Molucca. This photograph (**221**) of a terrorist's automatic rifle prodding through the curtains of a primary school is symbolic of the psychological brutality of terrorism everywhere. The Moluccans (described in one news despatch by an American journalist as the 'southern molluscs') were able to exert unusual pressure on the Dutch authorities because the country was then in the throes of a general election. In spite of this, and the international publicity that resulted, the Dutch at first played the crisis 'long', using a military psychiatrist to negotiate and bargain. After three weeks, peaceful persuasion was abandoned. The SAS offer of stun grenades was not taken up, but the methods used to break the siege were a model of those evolved by the Regiment: a carefully orchestrated assault using the shock effect of noise and smoke, as well as perfectly disciplined troops. Seven terrorists were arrested; two passengers and six terrorists aboard the train were

killed. One of these, the Palestinian-trained leader Max Papilaya, had been hit by 300 bullets. After the assault, the hull of the train resembled a pepperpot (**222**). By British standards, this was overkill.

223-225. This was the scene in the early morning darkness of Mogadishu Airport, Somalia, in October 1977 as 79 hostages fled to freedom from a Lufthansa Boeing airliner, which had been their flying prison and torture chamber for five macabre days. The German pilot, Juergen Schumann, had been murdered in front of the passengers and his body left on the floor of the aircraft during the last stage of the hijack, from Dubai. When these photographs were taken, the gun battle between the four terrorists — two men, two women — and men of West Germany's GSG-9 anti-terrorist squad was still raging. Two SAS soldiers, Major Alastair Morrison, OBE, MC, and Sergeant Barry Davies, BEM, were the first to smash into the fuselage from either side, using the Regiment's stun grenades. They carried no firearms. During the vital seconds of virtual deafness and blindness that paralysed the terrorists after the grenades had exploded, Morrison and Davies ducked away while fourteen of the German team swept into the aircraft. They roared at the passengers: 'Lie down!' In the eight-minute gun battle that followed, three out of the four terrorists were killed. The fourth, a woman, rolled two hand grenades down the aircraft floor, but these exploded harmlessly beneath padded passenger seats. In photograph **223**, passengers (including a group of German beauty queens) rush to

safety on the wing as one armed GSG-9 man stands guard by the door, while another encourages a frightened woman to leap to safety. In **224** more passengers crowd onto the wing while others (**225**) use ladders set against the trailing edge. Morrison (extreme left, arm raised) moves forward to help them. All four terrorists were Palestinians. Their leader, Zohair Akache, had assassinated three Yemeni officials in London six months previously. The terrorists were acting in this hijack on behalf of the imprisoned leaders of the West German Baader-Meinhoff group, who committed suicide after the failure of this attempt to obtain their release by blackmail. In that sense, the Mogadishu operation was a significant turning-point in the concerted European battle against international terrorism.

226. One of many victims of the Red Brigades, the Italian equivalent of the Baader-Meinhoff terrorist group in West Germany: this is the body of former Prime Minister Aldo Moro, the victim of almost two months' psychological torture during his captivity before he was finally murdered with eleven bullets. The Red Brigades, like chic revolutionaries elsewhere, talk a lot about 'the people', 'people's court' and 'the proletariat', but the vast majority of its members are spoiled youngsters of a privileged middle class; their leaders, dyspeptic academics. In common with other fascists, they have a psychopathic craving for power over other human beings.

227. During the search for Aldo Moro, a few months after Mogadishu, the SAS helped the Italians to create a new,

specialist anti-terrorist squad which was later to distinguish itself in the more successful search for the kidnapped American General James Dozier. The prolonged detention of General Dozier was brought to an end in January 1982 by this SAS-trained team, named the Nucleo Operativo Centrale di Sicurezza. NOCS comprises 30 men commanded by a 37-year-old colonel. In this photograph, the men wear balaclava masks in order to preserve their anonymity, a necessary precaution against assassination or terrorist pressure on them through their families. They are armed (foreground, kneeling) with Heckler & Koch assault rifles fitted with sniper-scopes; silenced Heckler & Koch MP5 submachine-guns (kneeling, extreme left, and standing, centre); and Italian Beretta Modello 12 submachine-guns (standing, right). The discovery of Dozier during an NOCS raid on a Verona flat, provided for a young woman student by her parents, cracked open many of the Red Brigades' secrets. It was followed, as a result, by the discovery of secret terrorist armouries and numerous arrests throughout Italy.

△228 ▽231

228-230. It was May 1980 before the SAS was called upon to perform publicly the techniques it had rehearsed in secret for seven years. By now, each of the Regiment's four squadrons was on stand-by for such an operation in turn, just as it was on the Irish rota. A quick-reaction CRW team was available at three minutes' notice. The rest of the squadron could follow very soon after. When the Iranian Embassy siege began, a new squadron had just taken over the long-awaited task of fighting terrorism on Britain's doorstep. The six terrorists sent to become martyrs for a hopeless cause — autonomy for one of Iran's most profitable oil zones — were naïve enough to believe that because Britain was a democracy it would be easily intimidated. Confident of success, the team went shopping for videos and other toys, which were then sent by air freight to Baghdad. Here (**228**), a terrorist appears at the embassy door to collect food supplies on the third day of the siege. But the negotiations did not proceed as expected. The terrorists spoke little English and their demands were sometimes relayed through their hostages, including (**229, 230**) PC Trevor Lock and Lebanese journalist Mustapha Karkouti. The terrorists demanded, again and again, negotiation with Downing Street through three Arab ambassadors. The British Government could not grant the terrorists this oblique, diplomatic recognition. Instead, they invited the ambassadors to join with them in persuading the terrorists to surrender, but made it clear that mediation by the ambassadors between the Government and the terrorists was out. Inside the embassy, as the delays in granting this demand lengthened, temperatures were rising dangerously.

231. A quarrel between the terrorist leader, Awn, and embassy press attaché Abbas Lavasani, a religious fanatic who objected to anti-Khomeni graffiti written on the embassy walls by the terrorists, precipitated the first death. Lavasani's murder was coldly efficient: three shots, all signalled to the police control room through the telephone link from the embassy. The dead man was then dumped on the embassy's front porch.

△232 ▽233

Covered by armed colleagues, detectives collected the body. The siege was now on the brink of disaster. Awn announced that he would murder one hostage every 45 minutes unless his demands were met. Inside, the hostages cowered and waited.

232, 233. Things now happened very fast. Control of operations was temporarily handed over to the SAS, which knew that it was a race against time if further murders were to be averted. From an adjoining balcony (**232**), one team placed a framed charge against an armoured window and blew it in. Then, wearing respirators to eliminate the effects of CS riot gas, and armed with Heckler and Koch submachine-guns — the same type of weapon used at Mogadishu — the soldiers threw themselves into the gloom inside (**233**).

234-236. Most of the hostages were being held at gunpoint in the room immediately above. The terrorist leader, Awn, was standing at the telephone discussing, he thought, arrangements for safe conduct out of the country. With him was PC Trevor Lock. As the assault party came in through the front window, a volley of CS gas cartridges was fired by the perimeter group. These, as in many cases in the United States, started a fire inside the building. While startled Metropolitan Police marksmen armed with pump-action shotguns watched, first the curtains, then the rest of the building blazed (**234**). One of the hostages was already fleeing towards the open window. Sim Harris, a BBC sound recordist was ordered to 'Get down!' as the first two SAS men stormed towards him. Soon afterward, afraid he might burn to death, he leapt to sanctuary (**235**) only to be bound up and passed from one soldier to another, down to the rear garden for identification. Harris wrote later: 'To them I owe my life'. Meanwhile, at the rear of the embassy, more soldiers were descending by abseil rope from the roof (**236**) while a third party smashed its way in through a hole dug from next door to within millimetres of the inner plaster. Inside the building, Awn was preparing to shoot one of the abseil group when PC Lock grappled with him. And, trapped on his rope, another soldier was severely burned as the fire swept through the embassy. He was cut loose, dropped to the balcony and killed an armed terrorist seconds later. The only hostage casualties were two men murdered by the terrorists, five of whom were killed by the SAS. The sixth terrorist went to prison. Democracy everywhere savoured the novelty of a victory over the pervasive threat of terrorism.

◁**236**

237-239. In the same week as the highly publicized Iranian Embassy operation, another siege was being broken by the SAS in Belfast. A team led by Captain Richard Westmacott, who had just joined the Regiment as a troop commander, attacked a house in Antrim Road occupied by eight members of the Provisional IRA, whose armoury included a powerful American M60 general purpose machine-gun (**237**). Westmacott was hit by a burst of fire from this gun as he led his men across the road from the team's 'Q-car'. He was the first SAS soldier to be killed by the IRA. In spite of this, the terrorists' white flag signal of surrender, as the rest of the SAS team smashed its way into the building with sledge-hammers, was accepted and honoured by the soldiers. As Westmacott's body lay in the road covered by a blanket (**238**), his killers were handed over to police custody for prosecution. Five weeks later they escaped from Crumlin Road prison. After a meeting with their solicitors, and on their way back to their cells, they produced pistols and then shot and bluffed their way out. In their absence they received prison sentences ranging from eighteen to thirty years. Photographs of seven of them (**239**) were released by the police. For Westmacott's murder, Fusco, Campbell, Doherty and Magee received life imprisonment, while Anthony Sloan, leader of the group, received twenty years. Campbell and one other escaper, Michael Ryan, were later recaptured and tried in the Irish Republic.

△237 ▽239

238▷

CAMPBELL, R.J.   SLOAN, Gerard,   McKEE, Michael A.   SLOAN, Anthony Gerar

...ZZ, Paul Patr.   FUSCO, Angelo   DOHERTY, Joseph P.T.   RYAN, Michael J.

△242

△243 ▽244

240-242. The SAS was formally committed to combat duty in Northern Ireland by Prime Minister Harold Wilson in January 1976, but there was a prelude to this commitment several years earlier. In 1969, when British troops came to the aid of beleaguered Catholics, 'D' Squadron of the SAS scoured the Antrim coast and glens for smuggled Protestant weapons, but none were found. Here, members of one of the search teams keep watch from a windswept Irish hillside (**240**). In Ireland their base was set in the bleak surroundings of Bessbrook, South Armagh (**241**). The customary rituals were observed, characteristic of SAS units everywhere from the jungle to the Arctic, including a brew-up in a sheltered spot (**242**). Squatting, foreground, is Nicolas Downie, a fourth-year medical student before he joined the SAS as a trooper. He now lives for months at a time with guerrillas in Afghanistan and elsewhere as a maker of award-winning television war documentaries. Within a few months of these photographs being taken, these men were fighting in Oman.

243, 244. By the time the SAS returned to Ulster in squadron strength in 1976, the IRA had become a formidable, well armed foe with clandestine training camps in the Irish Republic, and funds and weapons supplied from Warsaw Pact as well as United States sources. Photograph **243,** taken in 1976, shows two IRA guerrillas going into action to ambush a British Army patrol near Crossmaglen, South Armagh. One man (foreground) carries a vintage British Sten submachine-gun; the other is equipped with an American Armalite AR-18 selective-fire rifle, one of the most modern infantry weapons and one that the SAS itself has had difficulty in obtaining. With a muzzle velocity of about 3,250 feet per second and an effective maximum range of about 500 yards — more than a quarter of a mile — it is hardly the weapon of 'the weak against the strong'. Later, the IRA acquired an even heavier calibre automatic, the M60 general purpose machine-gun, seen here (**244**) before an admiring audience in Bogside, Londonderry. The man holding it is almost certainly Gerard Sloan, a member of the team that murdered Captain Westmacott. Sloan was sentenced in his absence for possessing the M60 'on another occasion' other than the murder. The M60 is a standard weapon with the US Army, Navy, Air Force and Marine Corps. It has an effective range of 2,250 yards. In 1978, when this photograph was taken, the price for a second-hand M60 was £750, while the 7.62mm×51 ammunition (the standard Nato infantry bullet) cost about £70 per thousand rounds. For British troops to use such a weapon in the close confines of a Belfast street — as the IRA used it — would be denounced as callous recklessness, similar to the use of Browning machine-guns by the Royal Ulster Constabulary in Belfast in 1969.

245. In the bandit border country of South Armagh, during the first year of its operations in 1976, the SAS rapidly created a 'no-go' area for the IRA. Four top terrorist leaders were either killed in action or taken prisoner, while six others fled deep into the Irish Republic for sanctuary. Immediately before the SAS arrived, 21 civilians had been murdered. These included ten unarmed Protestants taken from a bus at Bessbrook to be machine-gunned on the road. The secret of the SAS success was not just its readiness to shoot without hesitation at the right time, but its patient surveillance of known terrorist routes and the faces on them. Here, men of one such surveillance party, complete with sophisticated camera equipment, are recovered safely by helicopter after a rendezvous with other soldiers escorting them to the aircraft. Leading the party, but distinct from it, the surveillance team carries no visible weapons. One is bearded; the other laden with a bergen rucksack. The helicopter winchman, pointing to them, wants them on board first.

246. One of the most tragic undercover agents to work with the SAS in Northern Ireland was Captain Robert Nairac, Grenadier Guards, seen here among the young teenagers of Belfast, for whom he acquired an abiding affection. Nairac was a former pupil of the Roman Catholic Ampleforth College, North Yorkshire when the Abbot was Basil Hume, now Archbishop of Westminster. An Oxford boxing blue and history graduate, he approached Ireland's troubles with compassion and, some believe, the same romantic attachment that T. E. Lawrence had for the bedouin. He was never in the SAS, but his background and interest in the people led him into undercover intelligence work. His ability to impersonate the gruff, hard-drinking and wise-cracking Belfast Catholic was impressive, but he relied upon it too much for his own good. On the night of 14 May 1977, he arrived in a Republican bar near the border without an escort or

back-up party, disguised as a working man from faraway Belfast. He even sang a rebel song or two to an approving audience. But in South Armagh any stranger is suspect. He was asked to step outside and there a team of seven Provisional IRA men set upon him. He was taken away and repeatedly beaten up, almost escaping twice. By now his captors suspected that he was a member of the left-wing Official IRA, which has avoided political violence for years. An executioner was summoned from a bar across the border, but when he attempted to lead the British soldier away, Nairac, in spite of his now pitiful condition, seized the man's pistol. It misfired. Nairac was recaptured, executed and buried in an unmarked grave which has never been found. Those responsible for his murder were subsequently captured, convicted and imprisoned. His assassin admitted, 'He never told us anything'. In 1979, Nairac was awarded a posthumous George Cross.

247. After its initial success in South Armagh, the SAS was deployed over a wider area of the province. Wherever it went the tactics were the same: to use every snippet of information to prepare an ambush at the right place for the most dedicated IRA leaders and to capture them at a time when they were unquestionably conducting armed operations rather than talking to the media. One of the most wanted men in 1978 was Francis Hughes, a bandit-hero among his own people in the hills of South Londonderry near his home village of Bellaghy. Those who had to gather up the human remains of his booby-trap bomb victims — who included ten-year-old Lesley Gordon, a policeman's daughter — regarded Hughes as a psychopath. A few months after that murder, Hughes and two of his comrades walked into an ambush set up by the SAS but manned temporarily by soldiers of the Parachute Regiment. Because the IRA men wore combat jackets and carried modern weapons, the Paras mistook them for soldiers

of the Ulster Defence Regiment, came out of concealment, and spoke to them. They were immediately met by a hail of IRA bullets. One soldier was killed, but Hughes himself had been gravely wounded in the legs. He crawled away into the undergrowth and eluded search parties and tracker dogs for thirteen hours. When an SAS team found him, he said only, 'Your fucking dogs are no good'. As an RUC police officer put it later, 'Billy the Kid had nothing on this boy'. Having no licence to kill, or any wish to do so when this was patently unnecessary, the SAS men handed Hughes over to the police. He was treated for his wounds for eleven months in hospital. In time, he was imprisoned in The Maze, where he joined Bobby Sands, MP, in the 1981 hunger strike. He was the second man to die (after 59 days). Unlike Nairac, he was able to make a choice between life or death, even in captivity. And, unlike Nairac, his remains were available for a military funeral.

248, 249. In the 1980s, the use of the SAS as an invaluable instrument of diplomacy continued alongside its war against international terrorism, IRA terror and guerrilla warfare. Such operations rarely came to light, except by chance. One which did was the successful counter-coup in The Gambia in 1981. The ruler, President Jawara, was attending the wedding of Prince Charles in London when mutinous Army officers in The Gambia seized the main airport at Banjul, the capital, the national radio station and a number of hostages including the President's wives, children, courtiers, advisers and totally uninvolved fishermen. The coup was thought to have been engineered by Libya. Diplomatic relations between the two countries had been severed a few months before, after the discovery that Libyans were implicated in training a terrorist force in The Gambia. A very small SAS team travelled incognito to the country and freed the President's first wife, and her children, by posing as medical

orderlies in a clinic to which they were brought for treatment. The rebels' armed guard was overpowered and taken prisoner, and from that point onward the coup began to crumble. In their official capacity as advisers, the SAS men directed a highly professional assault on the mutineers' barracks six miles west of Banjul, backed up by loyal Gambians and friendly troops from neighbouring Senegal. In Britain the episode might have been worth no more than a paragraph or two, until a former SAS soldier, working in the country as a member of a British Army Training Team, recognized a familiar face and could not resist talking about what had happened. In the principal participant of the Royal Wedding — the Prince of Wales — the Regiment already had an old friend. It now had, in President Jawara, Charles's guest, a grateful client. The SAS kept well out of reach of cameras when these photographs were taken: wives and children of the President as they stroll contentedly out of captivity (**248**); mutineers, some with serious facial injuries, are led away to imprisonment after their surrender to the Senegalese (**249**).

Selection and training
The long, hard road

SAS selection and training are acknowledged to produce the world's most professional soldiers and, for that reason, the journalist's book of cliches usually describes them as supermen. This they are not. The SAS is a microcosm of the British Army. Its men are strong on endurance, which occasionally glows with a superhuman quality if survival is at stake. They are quick learners and they are robustly self-reliant. But these qualities, although they are increasingly rare in an urban society oriented towards sedentary work and passive recreation, are not unique to the SAS. Nor is another important characteristic, that of companionableness, a knack of living in close — sometimes very close — proximity with others in bad conditions, without serious loss of morale or performance.

What makes the SAS soldier unique is his combination of all these strengths with a dedication to learning and re-learning the art of war. It has been said that the SAS soldier going into action will select the exact array of weapons he needs in much the same way as a craftsman will choose the correct tools for a given job. An equally exact metaphor is that of the professional violinist in a string quartet, playing a limited repertoire, rehearsing endlessly and learning from the mistakes of one performance to create a flawless interpretation next time.

Basic selection for the regular, 22 SAS Regiment takes as its raw material soldiers serving in other units, such as Royal Engineers, as well as distinguished and more traditional fighting regiments. Before they start, the volunteers are given a scrupulous medical check, plus the Army's basic six-monthly fitness test. That test requires a man aged 30 to run 1½ miles, wearing boots, in twelve minutes. Up to ten per cent of volunteers are failed at this stage. What lies ahead of the rest is a finely tuned test of motivation and navigation on the Brecon Beacons and this, in extreme weather conditions, can prove fatal. Three victims in recent years succumbed to exposure resulting from over confidence in abnormal weather. All these men were physically fit. Another died in a fall. Their deaths underline the remorseless reality of all SAS training. The volunteer who is accepted is one who really wants to join the Regiment, above all else, and has probably trained hard before starting selection. As the course gets under way, two to three weeks are spent in marches across country using watch, map and compass in the punishing, windswept wilderness of the Beacons. The distances and weights carried increase daily, and the amount of rest time, including sleep, is gradually reduced; so is the number of volunteers still participating. After two weeks, each day's march is not less than fifteen hours and small injuries become more serious. The final week — the third for officers and the fourth for most soldiers — is Test Week. Instead of moving about in comforting and familiar groups, as soldiers usually do, the volunteers are working alone, against the clock. One typical day involves running three times up and down the remorseless, lung-tearing slopes of Pen-y-Fan and then, the same night, crossing an icy, dangerously fast River Wye at night, naked but carrying rucksack, rifle and clothes.

The ultimate test is the endurance march: 45 miles across country, blisters and all, carrying a 50lb pack, belt kit weighing another 12lb and an 18lb rifle which must be carried in the hand because most SAS weapons are not fitted with slings. It is the equivalent not of two marathons

250, 251. There was a time when the SAS believed in the 'numbered brick'. Such bricks were used to bring the weight of the bergen rucksack, now obsolescent, up to the required level during basic selection. The bricks were drawn from the quartermaster's store and, like other items of military hardware, they were carefully numbered. But that was also the era of the 'sickener' factor, when the end of a march was moved a mile or so down the road just as candidates thought they had reached the finishing post. Now, although the marches are just as hard, bricks — which fulfilled the useful function of simulating a load of ammunition — are replaced with extra clothing and other items of more obvious utility. Instead of sickeners, candidates are offered subtle encouragement to keep going by watchful instructors who loom up out of the rain and march some of the way with them. Their equipment is also changing. The compact load of the old triangular bergen (**250**), carried by this officer undergoing selection in April 1964, has given way to more bulk for the same weight used in today's rucksack (**251**).

but three, if the steepness of the terrain and the weight carried are taken into account. At the end of that journey, which must be completed in twenty hours, lies more training for those who qualify for temporary status with the Regiment. Among commissioned soldiers, Officers' Week involves making highly complex military judgements on insufficient information, or too much; stealthy reconnaissance of a target area, followed by an intimidating briefing delivered to an audience of SAS veterans who ask awkward questions. Next, for officers and men alike, come intensive introductory courses in medical, demolition and signals skills; weapon training; shooting; tactics; a combat survival course, including resistance to interrogation; six weeks in the jungle; and a parachute course.

The SAS recruit is now ready to be taught a specialized tactical skill. Each squadron is organized into separate troops, which concentrate on free-fall parachuting (a very different matter from basic, low-level static line military jumping); amphibious warfare, including scuba diving; mountaineering, including winter rock climbing and skiing; vehicle mobility, requiring astro-navigational skill in the desert, as well as extensive mechanical knowledge. Within each of these troops, each four-man patrol will have at least one whose personal, vocational skill is in medicine (including training in elementary surgery), or demolition and explosives, or as a linguist, or as a signaller.

Such a programme means that about two to three years are needed to turn a fully trained soldier into a basically qualified SAS soldier. Those who undertake additional specialist studies — for example, as a sniper or close-quarter battle marksman — will need even more time. For a long-serving SAS soldier, the process never ends. Unlike officers, who may spend no more than three years at a time wearing the coveted regimental beret, the rest can serve for as long as they are fit and willing to do so. Some men who join the Regiment as NCOs, subsequently obtain commissions and serve as SAS officers. Veterans of the Regiment are probably cross-trained specialists in several of the skills described above, as well as possessing a wealth of hard combat experience acquired in Aden, Borneo, Dhofar, Northern Ireland and elsewhere. When he is not in action, the SAS soldier will be evaluating new equipment or working as a member of an SAS training team almost anywhere in the non-Communist world, passing on his skills. He will be away from home eight months of the year.

Reservists in the Territorial Army serving with 21 SAS based in London or 23 SAS in the Midlands and north of England train for a more limited task. This is the vintage job of operating behind the lines in a European war. For them, the work-up period to selection test week is spread over many weekends, and the basic endurance march is 25 miles in 20 hours, inevitably below the standard required for regular selection. In spite of this, out of 1,400 recent volunteers for 21 SAS, only about ten finally made the grade. For those who do, virtually every weekend and numerous evenings have to be dedicated to the Regiment. Like the regulars, the reservists must also acquire basic tactical techniques, including parachuting. When SAS veterans assert that the Regiment's alternative motto is 'Who Trains Wins', they are not joking.

▽ 251

△252

△253

252, 253. From the beginning, selection is about soldiering and the tools of soldiering, as well as endurance and navigation. Here (**252**), volunteers for the Territorial SAS reserve strip and reassemble British 7.62mm L1A1 self-loading rifles in a timed test. Later, there are lectures in the use of foreign weapons, particularly those manufactured by the Eastern bloc (**253**).

254. As part of the continuation training for the tiny fraction of volunteers who pass basic selection, there is a combat survival course, including techniques of escape and evasion (how *do* you resist a police dog?) and resistance to interrogation after capture. These volunteers have been captured and put into blindfolds. Now they face an interrogation that stops short of physical brutality, which most SAS men regard as unproductive in real warfare, but which is long on psychological manipulation. In a real war, the SAS soldier has to resist the real thing if he is taken prisoner. His comrades' lives might depend upon the length of time he can hold out.

255-256. All SAS volunteers who have reached this stage go through the Army's basic parachute training course of eight jumps from about 800ft. First they learn the essentials from a training tower about 70ft high (**255**). Then comes the real thing, the parachute being opened automatically by a static line fixed to the aircraft (**256**).

257. The training now takes two parallel routes. The first of these is in an individual, vocational skill; the second, a specialized tactical technique. The 'vocational' subjects are usually a foreign language, field medicine, signalling or demolition work. Demolition artists learn to handle a variety of explosives, and targets, with confidence, ranging from railway tracks to trees. Why blow up trees? Because in the jungle it is the quickest way to clear a helicopter landing zone and, if a casualty has to be evacuated, time saves life. Numerous civilians, including women with difficult pregnancies, were evacuated by the SAS from the jungles of both Malaya and Borneo. Solid structures, such as buildings, come later in the course. The knowledge is useful when the only way to rescue hostages is to blast a way through to them.

△255 ▽256

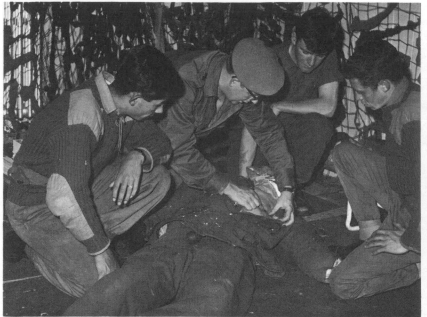

△258 △259

◁261 △262 △263 ▽264

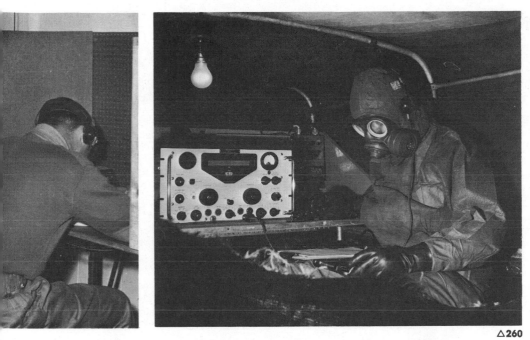

△260

△265

∧266   ▽267

258-260. An equally important vocational skill is basic field medicine. Here (**258**), volunteers learn with the help of an inflatable dummy to assess the seriousness of a bullet wound: whether a field dressing or evacuation to hospital (or the mortuary) will be most appropriate. It could be an important tactical decision. SAS 'bush doctors' have had to treat anything from pregnant women to sick camels. A good medic is worth his weight in gold. So is the signaller who can read Morse (**259**), a skill now limited almost exclusively to the SAS and the Royal Signals, many of whose men serve on attachment with the Regiment. The advantage of Morse is that with a minimum of primitive radio gear it can transmit signals in code over thousands of miles, unlike military voice transmitters. For high technology conflict in Europe, the signallers would have to operate equally well in the discomfort of nuclear, chemical and biological warfare known as 'noddy suits' (**260**).

261-265. What follows individual vocational training is work to acquire a group tactical skill; for example, in free-fall parachuting, mountaineering and rock climbing, amphibious warfare techniques, or cross-country (Mobility Troop) navigation in armed Land Rovers. The climbers tackle anything from a sheer rock face beneath an overhang (**261**) to an abseil from a mountain in Jordan alone or with a casualty (**262**); or from a parapet and high rope bridge in Corsica (**263, 264**). Mountain Troop people also include arctic warfare specialists who can ski (**265**), climb in ice or parachute onto it.

266. One exceptional feat in which two of the Regiment's men were involved was the assault on Everest in 1976. 'Bronco' Lane is seen here in pain as his frostbitten hands are exposed to heat after a night in a snow hole near the summit. Officially, this was 'adventurous training' and it cost him several mutilated fingers.

267. Equally ambitious was the Transglobe expedition organized by members of 21 SAS, led by Sir Ranulph Twistleton-Wykeham-Fiennes. This unique adventure circumnavigated the globe for the first time via the South and North Poles. Planning began in 1972 and the journey itself in 1979. The *Daily Mirror*'s Michael McCarthy reported from the North Pole in April 1982: 'They gave up everything for it. Jobs. Luxuries. Holidays. Security. Proper pay. Most poignant of all, children.' By now, Fiennes was accompanied by just one man, Charles Burton, though a 21 SAS back-up team elsewhere was exposed to much risk and hardship. In this photograph, Fiennes (left) and Burton celebrate at the North Pole. Time and again during a terrifying journey there, the ice cracked beneath their skidoo. The most perilous phase, across 500 miles of fragmenting Arctic Ocean ice, still lay ahead. Riding an ice floe on the Arctic drift, they were carried towards a rendezvous with a supply ship off Spitzbergen.

△268 △269

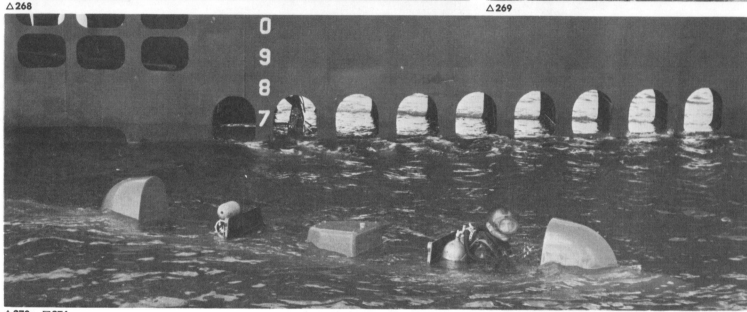

△270 ▽271

268-274. The men of Boat Troop, like those of the contemporary Special Boat Section (in post-war years, part of the Royal Marine Commando) have to be familiar with submarine operations. In **268** SBS men wait inside a submarine before surfacing. They emerge on deck and extract a collapsible, inflatable craft (**269**). When it is assembled — usually in darkness — the submarine will submerge and the commandos float away to make their own way ashore. (During the early days of the Falklands counterattack, SAS men used this method of infiltration into the Argentine occupied islands after they had parachuted into the Atlantic to rendezvous with the Royal Navy.) Cross-training with the US forces provides experience in the use of this sophisticated 'submersible vehicle' (**270**). For individual work in shallow waters there are even smaller craft (**271**). Basic SAS Boat Troop training uses armed Gemini inflatables like this one (**272**). Boat Troop people also mix pleasure with military business. Some, like this team from 21 SAS (TA), take to competitive canoeing (**273**) while others, in one of those elaborate jokes that keep boredom at bay, build the occasional raft, particularly when there is a competition with prizes at the end of it (**274**)

▽273

▽274

△275

△276

△278

△279 ▽280 ▽281

△277

275-277. The free-fall parachutists, even within the SAS, are a separate tribe within a tribe. Their training starts with a 60-second descent at 120mph from 12,000ft: an altitude to which only the most experienced civilian sports jumper will venture. Within a month or so, they are making descents from 25,000ft, wearing oxygen gear, in a descent which lasts two full minutes before the canopy opens at around 3,000ft. They jump with a 100lb bergen rucksack slung beneath the main parachute on the back, rifle strapped along the left side, carrying about the same weight as their own bodies. They dive out, in teams of four, and must follow a 300lb supply container known as 'The Bundle': an aerodynamically unpredictable beast, which can make a U-turn and rush back at them across the sky. To make that sort of descent at night, in cloud, with visibility restricted by ice on goggles and altimeters, requires a very special temperament, even among the elite of the SAS. Here, jumping in a more relaxed way, one regimental free-fall team makes a poised, pirouette exit off the Hercules ramp (**275**) while another (**276**) dives off. All the men are in 'clean fatigue', without extra military equipment or 'The Bundle'. Fully equipped for military free-fall (**277**), this is how the soldier appears.

278-281. On the face of it, Mobility Troop, in armed Land Rovers, have a slightly calmer existence (**278**) . . . Or so it seems, until the vehicle has to be extracted from a tree into which it has been parachuted, or from dense undergrowth (**279**); perhaps even from a sand sea in Iran (**280**). In Canada some years ago, Mobility Troop also experimented with motor cycles as vehicles suitable for SAS use. Possibly, they had in mind the use to which the Rhodesian Selous Scouts put them as cross-country pursuit vehicles. During the war that preceded the creation of Zimbabwe, the tracker rode pillion to spot the guerrillas' spoor, shouting directions to the driver. The SAS was content to test the ruggedness of the machines with solo riders on firm going and in the wet (**281**).

282. At the end of this exhaustive training, the array of experience and skill combined within a typical 22 SAS four-man patrol is represented by this group, on exercise in the Cameron Highlands, Malaysia, in 1970. Left to right:

Trooper C. The medic, aged 25, from Boat Troop. He has five years' SAS service; trained as a parachutist for 'wet jumps' into the sea and is also a canoeist, boatman and diver trained as a frogman. He has completed a coastal navigation course. He refreshes his medical training by spending one month a year in the casualty department of a major British hospital in a big city. His alternative specialization is as a signaller. He speaks Malay and concentrated on 'hearts and minds' work during the Borneo campaign.

Corporal B. Patrol commander, aged 30, from the Free Fall Troop. With almost seven years in the SAS, he is also a trained signaller and 'bush doctor' to advanced level. He is expert in undetected entry into enemy territory through nocturnal free-fall. He has attended sabotage leader and free-fall courses with the French and American armies; and qualified as advanced driver and vehicle mechanic. He speaks Malay and Arabic.

Trooper M. Tracker and head scout, aged 27, from Mountain Troop. In his five years with the SAS, he has trained in winter warfare at French, German and Norwegian army schools and is qualified as a dry and wet rock climber to 'Very Severe' standard. He is also a trained signaller and demolition specialist. He speaks French and has just qualified with the German Mounted Division as a ski instructor.

Trooper H. Patrol signaller, aged 23 and on his first SAS tour, serving with Mobility Troop in Land Rovers. He is an advanced driver and vehicle mechanic and has completed his astro-navigation training. He is learning a foreign language. By SAS standards, he is a comparative beginner.

△ 283

△ 284 ▽ 285

283-287. As well as training their own men, SAS instructors travel the world to act as tutors to Allied armies, where their presence is a useful tool of British diplomacy. Here, members of the Bermuda Militia Artillery receive instruction in canoe patrolling (**283**) from two members of a four-man SAS training team. In London, actress Julie Ege – about to spend a few days in isolation on a Caribbean Island – is given access to a briefing by 21 SAS (TA) on survival (**284**) and is then measured up for a combat suit (**285**). In Kenya (**286**), pupils demonstrate what they have learned about removing enemy sentries, silently. Few foreign armed services have anything to teach the SAS, but the Americans are an occasional exception. There is a free interchange of information and training methods between the British and US Special Forces, which benefits both in spite of major differences of approach to similar problems. Here (**287**), a small arms expert of the US Special Forces gives a lecture to SAS soldiers.

SELECTION AND TRAINING   115

Exercises
Risk without glory

The exercises undertaken by the SAS, in which they apply the training and use the techniques described in the previous section, range from the pleasantly irrelevant to the terrifyingly realistic. At one end of the scale is the sort of thing that gives rise to a joke about identifying SAS men in Nato exercises as 'those who approach a snowfield and walk through it backwards'. At the other are 'training-operations' in which what starts as an exercise in a potential combat zone turns into the real thing. Malaya and South Arabia are cases in point. Such are the risks involved in SAS methods — however nicely calculated — that they are as potentially fatal as real warfare. The Regiment is not complacent about such risks. It measures them carefully and takes them if the results will be worth it. What is surprising is not that there are some serious casualties from time to time, but that these are so rare.

Philip Warner, in his account of the Regiment, writes of an exercise in Denmark in which a frozen lake barred the path of a patrol. 'Unfortunately it was not frozen very hard

and if it cracked there was a fair chance that the patrol would disappear until their bodies were found the following spring. It began to creak. They could have turned back. After all it was only a Territorial Army (reservist) exercise. Their leader — a young millionaire . . . — had decided that if you were doing an exercise you should take it with all its implications; they went on.'

In common with the Royal Marine Commando, the SAS frequently plays the role of enemy to Allied forces. This gives the Regiment a chance to rehearse its skills in infiltration into hostile territory. During the big Nato exercise 'Crusader' in the autumn of 1980, men from 21 and 23 SAS (TA) repeatedly penetrated headquarters hundreds of miles behind the notional front line. Sometimes they created mild havoc with Thunderflash firecrackers. Occasionally, they took over traffic control and misdirected Nato reinforcement convoys off their correct routes and into rural tracks leading nowhere. More frequently they crept into someone's inner sanctum to deposit leaflets announcing the visit,

▽288

▽289

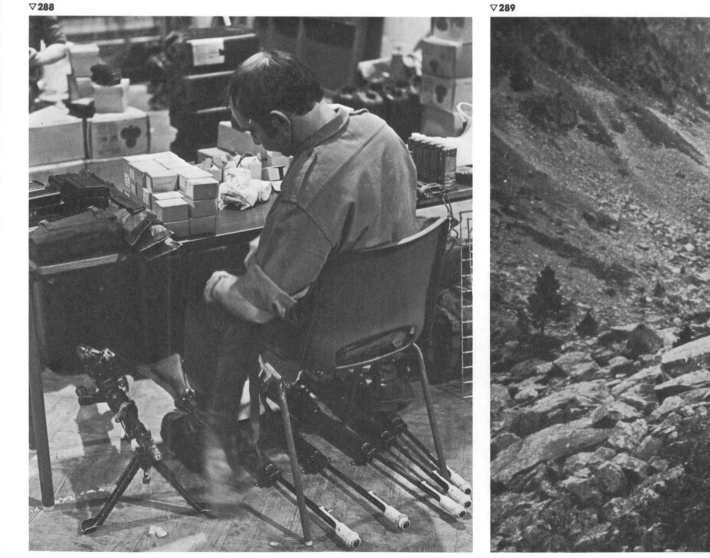

promising 'We will be back'. One of the most effective — and, for the victim embarrassing — visits of this sort was paid on a general, a divisional commander, as he caught up on some well earned sleep.

In another episode, an attempt by the Royal Military Police to halt an SAS team after a raid on its headquarters was overcome by the simple but expensive expedient of driving the patrol's Land Rovers through the RMP road-block — which also consisted of Land Rovers. No doubt there were some hard official words about the episode, just as there were about the sudden deaths of a number of Danish police dogs sent out to stop an SAS patrol. But the SAS is not in the business of training for real war by cutting awkward corners with the aid of 'exercise artificiality'. That notion is left to the military umpire, if he can move fast enough to see what the Regiment is actually doing.

Other SAS exercises take the Regiment around the world to co-operate with Allied armies and to refresh expertise in the jungle, the desert, or some other wilderness. Such environmental training might or might not have an eventual exercise plot — an attack on an airfield, for example — but this is probably less important than the use of a hard natural theatre in which to march, survive and still be fit to fight. With the growth of international terrorism, in particular the evolution of hostage-taking as a tool of terrorism, the SAS has also conducted many exercises with police forces in Britain and security forces elsewhere. After-wards there is a very careful analysis of what happened and, in Britain, whether the Regiment's rescue team could be accused of using more than 'minimum force' to achieve its objective. Such links are strengthened by training a small number of police teams in SAS siege-busting methods at the Regiment's base camp. The response of most policemen, see-ing the SAS in action for the first time, is somewhat like that of the Duke of Wellington on surveying elements of his army in the Peninsular: 'I don't know what effect these men will have upon the enemy, but, by God, they terrify me!'

288. Every exercise begins with the ritual of drawing equipment. For the quarter-master, who issues it, it is like riding an organizational tidal wave. Here, at the headquarters of 23 SAS (TA), the equip-ment begins to flow in preparation for a big exercise in western Europe. All weapon barrels are stopped and marked with white tape to prevent the accidental discharge of live ammunition, though the guns can still fire blanks.
289. Even for the 'weekend soldiers' of 21 SAS, exercises take them into unfamiliar and potentially dangerous terrain. Here, such soldiers march through the Pyrenees after parachuting into the area.

△290 ▽291

△292 ▽293 294▷

290-293. Some of these reservists who went into the wilderness of British Columbia were ambitious enough to carry everything, including the kitchen sink (**290**). This becomes less feasible at river crossings — and there are many rivers in British Columbia — whether by log bridge (**291**) or — using a recognized SAS technique for keeping clothes dry — by ford (**292**). At the end, the result is sometimes almost total exhaustion (**293**).
294. The regular regiment, 22 SAS, travels to even more exotic places as a matter of routine, with no time to acclimatize before starting work. Here in a remote area of the Cameron Highlands, Malaysia, Regimental Sergeant Major Lawrence Smith, MC, one of the most respected regimental veterans, charms a group of aboriginal children. During Confrontation in Borneo in 1965,

Smith was responsible for the longest area of front in the campaign, on the Sarawak border. A Gurkha history relates: 'He personally led several dangerous and exacting operations when detailed preliminary reconnaissance reports were needed.' His organization of covering fire for a Gurkha party ambushed by an Indonesian company saved the group, after which he went into the jungle by helicopter to bring out a seriously wounded soldier whose leg was saved as a result.

295-297. The Middle East has long been a training ground as well as a war zone for SAS soldiers, and in this respect they have much to teach American special forces now recruited into the US Rapid Deployment Force. In Jordan, the Regiment had the task of 'attacking' an isolated fort straight from the pages of Beau Geste (**295**) after a long journey across the desert. The attack goes in by night. As a signal pistol is fired, rocket launchers open up (**296**) and the fort is hit by streams of tracer (**297**).

298-300. The United Arab Emirates, in the Arabian Gulf, is another familiar exercise area, particularly useful for desert driving and survival by Mobility Troop. Here (**298**) in Sharjah, such a group sets itself up for a photograph that seems to suggest 'Anything Stirling can do, we can do better'. The Land Rovers used are known, after the colour of their camouflage, as 'Pink Panthers'. In the desert hills, a simulated but exhausting manhunt ends in this capture (**299**). Since this is 22 SAS, the weapons have no slings and must be carried in the hand. The weapons are in firing order. The same exercise provides mortar practice with live ammunition (**300**).

301-303. The Regiment was involved in a prolonged exercise in Sharjah shortly before it went to war in Oman. Desert driving — a highly specialized art in which every crest has to be crossed, if possible, at right angles — was prominent. In **301** the camera catches the exhilaration of the desert wind in the face and the giddy sense of freedom of desert life. Such euphoria was often misplaced. As a precaution against soft going over the next ridge, before it was too late to change direction, the driver's mate had to jump out of the 'Pink Panther' (Land Rover) and run to the top (**302**). When such precautions were not taken, the result was a sudden lurch (**303**) and a vehicle which could only be dug out with much care and hard work.

△295

△298   ▽301 ▽302

△296 △297

△299 △300 ▽303

△304   △305 ▽306

△307 ▽308

304, 305. In the absence of a real enemy, exercises also give the Regiment a chance to experiment in various ways, including the use of local transport. This camel patrol (**304**) in 1968 lasted three weeks. Some of those involved had already experienced the charm of riding shaggy mountain ponies in the mountainous forests of Norway (**305**).

306, 307. Resupply for exercises in such remote areas is as real as during warfare itself. Indeed, one of the purposes of such exercises is to experiment with methods of doing this. During the big exercise in Sharjah in 1969—70, some material was dropped by parachute (**306**) while at other times the Beaver, the aerial work-horse of deserts hot and cold, moved people as well as material. The aircraft was greeted informally (**307**).

308-310. Every exercise environment has its problems. In Brunei, these range from sharing a hole in the ground, among the insects (**308**), to a rope bridge which gives less support (**309**) than it promised. For the medic, seen here (**310**) administering an injection to someone who already has an injured knee, it is business as usual whether the war is real or not.

311. Within the Nato area — extending from Arctic Norway to southern Turkey and soon, most probably, to include Spain — the SAS has a variety of jobs. The regular regiment, 22 SAS, tends to concentrate its efforts in the wilder areas of the northern and southern flanks and — for training purposes — the Bavarian mountains. Here in Greece, a senior officer joins some of his men in the field in the mundane task of potato bashing. They talk; he listens.

▽309

▽310

▽311

△312 ▽313

312-316. In Germany it is the two Territorial units, 21 and 23 SAS, that exercise most frequently with a small cadre of regular instructors seconded from 22 SAS. The most important job on such exercises is reconnaissance (**312**), and for that to be successful the soldier must remain close to the ground and virtually invisible. British SAS soldiers also train in conjunction with Allied Special Forces, such as this Belgian team (**313**). When a patrol moves out of cover, like this group taking over an isolated farmhouse (**314**), it does so at a sprint, with the first men inside instantly turning to cover the backs of their comrades as they advance. Although constantly on the move under cover to avoid detection, the Morse signaller (**315**) still has to maintain contact with the unit's headquarters. The end of the first phase of an exercise (**316**), and one man quenches his considerable thirst before passing the water to his exhausted comrades.

△314　▽315

▽316

317, 318. One of the great exercise artificialities is the presence of various sorts of professional spectators, including umpires, journalists and film crews. In **317** one such crew explains to men of 21 SAS roughly what it has in mind. Not all cameramen are welcomed. This soldier (**318**) offers a Chinese gesture that is unlikely to be copied by more august personages who have trouble with paparazzi.

319-321. There are some exercises that have little to do with warlike preparation and much to do with the Regiment's potential for aiding the civil authorities. During the blizzards of January 1982, SAS soldiers provided vehicles and drivers capable of carrying sorely needed medical supplies from the north of England to a hospital near the Regiment's base at Hereford. In the late 1960s, serious flooding in the area put local livestock at risk. Men of 22 SAS — particularly Boat Troop — provided assistance in rescuing people, sheep (**319**) and other livestock. This soldier (**320**) wore his wet suit to recover a stranded, hungry horse. Most SAS men have known worse, like this soldier examining the debris left by a flood which deluged his patrol during an exercise in Malaya (**321**).

322. Very rarely, the boot is on the other foot and the civil authorities come to the aid of the SAS. One such occasion was during a serious fire at the Regiment's Bradbury Lines barracks.
323. Exercises of whatever sort end with a careful debriefing of the soldiers involved by an officer, as in this picture. It is a time of tension for the soldiers involved, when mistakes are revealed. Since they frequently play the role of enemy, their reports often conflict with those of their by now angry opponents, and umpires do not see everything.

△319

△320

Ritual
(and other tribal customs)

Every British regiment has its own, peculiar customs, from the Greenjackets' habit of drilling with the rifle at the trail to the Gloucesters' fondness for a cap badge on the back of the beret. Most SAS soldiers are seeking an escape from such ritual. SAS regimental customs, such as they are, reflect the no-nonsense, down to earth quality of the men in it, and are rich in both scepticism and black humour. Rejection of 'big timing', or undue pomp and ceremony, buttons, insignia and badges of rank runs deep in the SAS character. John Lodwick, writing about the Regiment in the 1940s, describes how he arrived to join the Regiment wearing the uniform and shoulder flashes of the Army Commando, and walked into the office of one of the veterans. 'I was still wearing the badges of my previous unit. They were numerous, they were garish, they were large. I made the mistake of walking into Bill Cumper's office. "My God, look out . . . the commandos are here", he shouted, and diving for his Luger, attempted to shoot out the lights.'

Like most things connected with the Regiment, an SAS 'custom' — the very word suggests a way of thought alien to the most pragmatic regiment in the British Army — has to serve an obviously useful purpose. One of these is the 'Dead Man's Auction'; the sale of items of personal equipment belonging to a soldier who has been killed while serving with the SAS, to his surviving comrades. Outrageous prices are charged for mundane articles, and the funds that result are passed on to the dead soldier's next-of-kin.

SAS soldiers delight in competition, and each generation serving in the Regiment will usually start some new way of testing one another. In the 1960s, before Operation 'Storm' began in Dhofar, it was free-fall parachuting. More recently, marathon running has become fashionable, with some soldiers running ten miles before they start a routine day's work and another ten miles after it. To a greater degree than most, SAS soldiers are exposed to periods of boredom in isolated parts of the world, and the stress of danger. The first — being intelligent, hyperactive people — they relieve through elaborate jokes; the second, with a therapeutic drinking party when the time is right.

Parades on the whole are not popular and mindless foot drill entirely unknown. In this, there are times when an SAS centre can be deceptively civilian in style and tone. Soldiers address officers as 'Boss' rather than 'Sir', and even the

324. It was Christmas Day in the jungle — the Malayan jungle, 1956 — when an SAS team from 'D' Squadron dressed for the occasion. The date on the calendar, in fact, was 27 December. Christmas dinner was planned by a member of the patrol who had been an Army commando, Foreign Legionnaire, and a professional cook. One of those present, David Kirby, recorded in his diary, 'Pat and Arthur have produced the most text-book oven out of manpack frames, ration pack tins, stream-bed boulders and concrete of sand and sanitary lime. . . . Eric has made a dickie and bow tie and cuffs to dress for dinner — the abos must be flummoxed by it all . . .' Eric Wright did not neglect to wear his cartridge belt or carry his pump-action shotgun. A thoroughly traditional Christmas dinner was rounded off with 'rum punch . . . pum runch . . . pun rumch . . . Eee! It were a good do!'

325, 326. A celebration of another sort during a 'D' Squadron exercise in Jordan in 1971: one of the Regiment's most ingenious interrogators and practical jokers organized his team to construct an instant artillery piece consisting of drainpipe and pieces of wood. An exercise Thunderflash provided the bang (**325**). Meanwhile, finding a mock tank, another SAS soldier announced that the Afrika Korps was back in business — long after Stirling had thought he had finished it off — and was taking over the country (**326**).

327. Among both the regular soldiers of 22 SAS and the volunteer Territorials there is a common fondness for celebrating the end of a war, or an exercise. Men of 21 and 23 SAS modestly celebrated their survival in British Columbia with 60 dozen beers, all neatly assembled beside a Canadian lake for proper disposal.

324▷

'Boss' has a touch of irony. Conversations are conducted in an atmosphere of equality, so much so that one Cabinet minister, visiting 22 SAS, later accused his hosts of dressing up an officer as a lance-corporal in an effort to impress. The man concerned was a lance-corporal. But beneath the surface, an SAS establishment is an extraordinarily efficient machine in which weapons and vehicles are kept in top class condition for the same reason the men keep themselves in the same state: they are self-starting professionals in their business who do not need a time clock, or a muster parade, to be on the start line and ready to begin work. For those who do not match up, there is the ultimate and dreaded sanction of being posted away from the SAS and back to the soldier's original unit. When an 'RTU' (return to unit) order is made, the offender and his personal gear are moved out within an hour or so. This ruthless despatch of failures is another of the very few SAS rituals.

Among the Territorial regiments, 21 SAS has a special problem. It is, technically, still the Artists' Rifles. With that historic title it has inherited an annual commitment to parade at the Royal Academy of Art in London's Piccadilly. From time to time it is persuaded to participate at other ceremonial functions in the City. It meets such commitments honourably but, one suspects, with less enthusiasm than most other tasks. RSM Lawrence Smith, MC, asked to define the SAS, said, 'The SAS is the soldier'. This section portrays that soldier going about his domestic business both in mourning and celebration.

△325　　　　　　　▽327　326▷

△328

△329

◁332   △333

▽334

335▷

△330　331▷

328-331. It was in 1970 when a youthful Prince of Wales first visited 22 SAS at Hereford. In **328** he is seen with officers then serving with the Regiment, including Major Alastair Morrison, closely followed by one of the Regiment's most famous soldiers, Lieutenant-Colonel (now Lieutenant-General) John Watts, at that time Commanding Officer of 22 SAS. Brigadier Fergus Semple brings up the rear. It was on the same occasion that the prince inspected a four-man patrol after it had given a display of abseil techniques (**329**). Afterwards, he and Princess Anne joined senior NCOs in their mess for a drink (**330**). The Regiment left for Oman soon after these photographs were taken. For these military pensioners of the Royal Hospital, Chelsea (**331**), the Regiment's hospitality included a demonstration of unarmed combat.

332-335. It is rare for the SAS to parade in public. When the Regiment was granted the Freedom of Hereford, recently, for example, there was little public show. Some of the more memorable include this occasion in wartime Italy (**332**), when the SAS paraded jointly with partisans; or this display by the Greek 'Sacred Squadron', a year or so earlier, in Lebanon after ski training (**333**). At the end of the war in Europe, the French SAS squadron turned out with tommy-guns to parade formally on its transfer to the army of France (**334**). These days, the only comparable event is the 21 SAS parade — as the Artists' Rifles — at the Royal Academy of Art. Some men came dressed for Arctic warfare (**335**).

△336

▽340

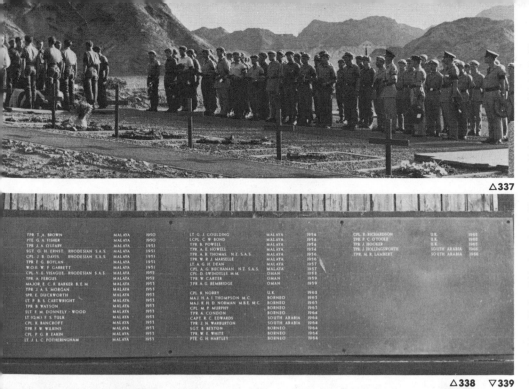

△337

TPR T. A. BROWN | MALAYA 1950
PTE G. A. FISHER | MALAYA 1950
TPR J. A. CLEARY | MALAYA 1951
SGT O. H. ERNST RHODESIAN S.A.S. | MALAYA 1951
CPL J. B. DAVIS RHODESIAN S.A.S. | MALAYA 1951
TPR F. G. BOYLAN | MALAYA 1951
W.O.II W. F. GARRETT | MALAYA 1951
CPL V. E. VISAGIE RHODESIAN S.A.S. | MALAYA 1951
TPR A. FERGUS | MALAYA 1952
MAJOR E. C. R. BARKER B.E.M. | MALAYA 1953
TPR J. A. S. MORGAN | MALAYA 1953
SPR E. DUCKWORTH | MALAYA 1953
LT P. R. S. CARTWRIGHT | MALAYA 1953
TPR B. WATSON | MALAYA 1953
SLT F. M. DONNELY-WOOD | MALAYA 1953
LT (QM) F. S. TULK | MALAYA 1953
CPL K. BANCROFT | MALAYA 1953
TPR F. W. WILKINS | MALAYA 1953
CPL P. G. R. EAKIN | MALAYA 1953
LT J. L. C. FOTHERINGHAM | MALAYA 1953

LT G. J. GOULDING | MALAYA 1954
LCPL C. W. BOND | MALAYA 1954
TPR R. POWELL | MALAYA 1954
TPR A. E. HOWELL | MALAYA 1955
TPR A. R. THOMAS. N.Z. S.A.S. | MALAYA 1956
TPR W. R. J. MARSELLE | MALAYA 1956
LT A. G. H. DEAN | MALAYA 1957
CPL A. G. BUCHANAN. N.Z. S.A.S. | MALAYA 1957
CPL D. SWINDELLS M.M. | MALAYA 1958
TPR W. CARTER | OMAN 1959
TPR A. G. BEMBRIDGE | OMAN 1959

CPL R. NORRY | U.K. 1962
MAJ H. A. I. THOMPSON M.C. | BORNEO 1963
MAJ R. H. D. NORMAN M.B.E. M.C. | BORNEO 1963
CPL M. P. MURPHY | BORNEO 1963
TPR A. CONDON | BORNEO 1964
CAPT R. C. EDWARDS | SOUTH ARABIA 1964
TPR J. N. WARBURTON | SOUTH ARABIA 1964
SGT B. BEXTON | BORNEO 1964
TPR W. E. WHITE | BORNEO 1964
PTE G. H. HARTLEY | BORNEO 1964

CPL R. RICHARDSON | U.K. 1965
TPR P. C. O'TOOLE | U.K. 1965
TPR J. HOOKER | U.K. 1967
TPR J. HOLLINGWORTH | SOUTH ARABIA 1966
TPR M. R. LAMBERT | SOUTH ARABIA 1966

△338   ▽339

336-338. There are more private, bleak occasions when the Regiment mourns the loss of its men collectively, as on this misty Remembrance Day at the Hereford barracks (**336**); or individually, as at the funeral of a Radfan casualty in 1966 (**337**). By tradition, the names of SAS men killed in action are inscribed on the base of a regimental clock, a practice that began after the Regiment was raised afresh in 1950 (**338**). To stay alive, in SAS jargon, is to 'beat the clock'.

339. Another, unique commemoration takes place at Moussey in France. In an area close to the German border, SAS soldiers operating behind German lines were frequently betrayed by French informers motivated either by fear or gain. The modest village of Moussey was an exception and it paid for its loyalty. As a reprisal for the sanctuary and food provided for SAS soldiers, the Nazis removed most of the male population to concentration camps and shot others. Few survived this massacre. The bodies of SAS casualties are buried in the local churchyard, which is an official war cemetery. In this photograph, men from 21 SAS parade through the village on their way to the war memorial.

340, 341. Finally, there is the sort of picture that appears in countless albums, the group photograph. These two photographs represent the post-war SAS coming of age. Picture **340** depicts Calvert's original Malayan Scouts, 'A' Squadron drawn from a variety of units and still clad in their original uniforms. The only SAS symbol in view is on a hastily constructed regimental shield. In 1965, a free-fall parachute team, drawn from 22 SAS at Hereford, set a British altitude record, and some of its members went on to represent Britain in international competition (**341**). Several of them profoundly influenced the evolution of the civilian sport in Britain. More important, they were hard, responsible soldiers.

▽341

The Australians
Special forces unlimited

Britain has the SAS, the Royal Marine Commando, including the SBS and other specialist forces. Australia has only one, and that is the Australian Special Air Service Regiment. This means that the Australian SAS has unequivocal coverage of such operations, including amphibious and submarine tasks that would normally be the prerogative of the SBS in Britain.

The unit was raised at Campbell Barracks, Swanbourne, Western Australia in 1957. By then, the Malayan campaign, in which the New Zealand as well as the British SAS regiments figured so prominently, was almost finished. The Australian SAS had a modest start as a company (about 120 men) of the Royal Australian Regiment until the Borneo Emergency began in 1962, after which the unit was expanded into a full-blown regiment. This change was formally completed on 4 September 1964, the anniversary of Australia's first combined operation — land, sea, air — in the war against the Japanese, an operation mounted in 1943 in New Guinea. During the intervening four years, the Australian SAS was picking up hard experience on exercises in Thailand, New Guinea and Okinawa. After its evolution as a regiment, the unit continued to expand until by 1966 it had three fighting 'Sabre' squadrons, a regimental HQ, base squadron and elements of 151 Signals Squadron attached to it. On that scale, it rivalled its British parent.

In 1965, 1 SAS Squadron went to Brunei. The initial rising there had been stifled three years before, and the main action had moved to the frontier between Malaysian Borneo and the Indonesian zone known as Kalimantan. Subsequently, 2 SAS served in the Kuching area, on the coast of Sarawak, where the British SAS headquarters was established for a time. It was also near the border with Kalimantan and, although it is long since a matter of history that British forces led by SAS guides engaged in carefully controlled cross-border operations, the Australian defence establishment has never confirmed that its new SAS Regiment was permitted to take part in these.

Simultaneously, the Regiment was committed to the war against Vietcong forces in Vietnam. From 1966 until 1972, the three fighting squadrons served in rotation in the Phuoc Tuy province, south-east of the capital, Saigon. With the British regiment committed on a similar basis to South Arabia (Aden and Radfan) as well as Borneo, it meant that SAS warriors, for a brief period, were simultaneously engaged in three entirely separate armed conflicts: in Vietnam, in Borneo, and in South Arabia.

The Australian SAS performance in Vietnam won praise from its allies. To be sure, some of its men were engaged — like the much smaller New Zealand troop operating alongside the Australians — in the classic SAS tasks of deep reconnaissance and ambush. But an entirely new light on the Australian SAS role in that war was shed by a film made with official blessing, entitled 'The Odd Angry Shot'. The film did not reach a substantial British audience until 1981, when it was screened on television as part of an Australian film festival. There was much that was familiar to British students of the SAS, notably the wry humour, quick intelligence and low tolerance of boredom. The fighting role that was projected, however, was more orthodox. It was that of a mobile 'fire brigade' reserve, ready to move out in Chinook helicopters at a few minutes notice, and then to march into something approaching pitched battle with the enemy. A British SAS observer compared this to the role and style of, say, the UK's Parachute Regiment rather than the cunning, low-profile 'keeni-meeni' operations in which the New Zealand and British SAS had become specialists.

Like all of Australia's armed forces, the SAS has to justify its existence and utility by reference to the strategy of the region in which it functions. In a vast, yet remote region, such justification is not as obvious as it is in, say, the confrontational environment of Europe. No sensible government with a vast, wealthy yet still under-populated country in an overcrowded and hungry hemisphere would trust to luck for its security, however. The SAS, with its cost effective mixture of high mobility and low numbers, provides Canberra with a peculiarly valuable quick response to any threat which could arise in foreseeable circumstances.

According to one SAS authority, only the Regiment possesses the mobility and experience to train and lead local citizens' militia to respond to landings at several widely separated points around Australia's enormous coastline. Hitherto, for good historical reasons, Australia has looked north to contemplate the possibility of trouble. Yet, incredible as it might have seemed a short time ago, the first British offensive action since 1956 (Suez) has now taken place at South Georgia, on the edge of Antarctica. That uninhabited zone is now one more place — possibly the last zone of peace — to which the military planners must now turn their attention and is one which inevitably involves Australian interests even if, so far, military action has been on the other side of the Antarctic continent, away from Australia's research stations. There is nothing to suggest that the Australian SAS has had to study Arctic (or Antarctic) warfare techniques so far, though the Australian Army does have a surprisingly useful ski team that takes part in downhill races in Europe. The evidence of the photographs in this section, supplied by the Australian SAS itself, suggests that — as one would expect — it is still training for operations nearer home, in jungle, bush and veldt country. This does not mean that the Australians, together with their New Zealand cousins, will be reluctant, if the need arises, to adapt to extremes of cold. The British SAS has at least one case on record of a bandaged veteran in Aden, asked by an inspecting officer the nature of his injury, who truthfully replied: 'Frostbite, sir'. He had arrived fresh from a particularly hard time in Arctic Norway.

△342   ▽343

342. Among the banana trees and flies of North Queensland in conditions not unlike those of Vietnam, an Australian patrol carries British-style SLR rifles with no slings. This is an exercise. If the patrol had been operational, it is unlikely that the men would be without rucksacks, equipped only with belt kit, in a wilderness in which the main back-pack would be hard to retrieve, once cached. Faces and arms, without camouflage paint, reflect light and make the soldier a ready target.

343. A standard 10ft assault craft leading another well laden flat-bottomed vessel in conditions strongly reminiscent of Borneo. But again, the high profile of the men involved, notably the signaller, suggests an exercise back home in Australia.

△344 △345 △346 △347 △348

344-348. The difference between a basic exercise in Australia and a simulated operational patrol in Vietnam is clear from this picture (**344**) of fire and movement training. Equipment, including camouflage uniforms, is new and unmarked as are the rucksacks. An exposed wrist, without camouflage, shines like a bandage. But the American Armalite rifles and the camouflage sweat rag worn round the head all reflect the Vietnam experience. Pre-Vietnam training in Australia included the essential drill of clearing the helicopter at speed (**345**) and going to earth as rapidly as moles (**346**). In jungle warfare, it is the moment of greatest vulnerability. This patrol on exercise (**347**) is armed with a mixture of SLR and Armalite rifles. The Australian SAS used both in Vietnam. Like the British SAS, the Australians have also taken an interest in the motor cycle for rapid penetration of mountain and broken bush country, a lesson picked up from the war in Rhodesia/Zimbabwe. This soldier (**348**) is armed with a silenced Sterling sub-machine-gun, an ambush weapon which, presumably, would give the attacker time to flee after hitting his target. Australian trials with motor cycles have preserved the four-man unit. Each group of four machines is aided by one support and maintenance vehicle. This group of photographs provides only the most basic profile of the Australian SAS which, because of its significant amphibious role, has to be among the most versatile of the world's special forces. Most of the skills described elsewhere in this volume, including diving and free-fall parachuting, are routinely employed by the Australians. Cross-training with the British and Americans means that they keep up to date with the latest lessons of real combat. The arrangement is reciprocal. During and after the Vietnam War, Australian veterans of that campaign became instructors at the British Jungle Warfare School in Malaysia.

The New Zealanders
In at the beginning

New Zealand has a special place in the history of the SAS. While it is true that both Australia and Rhodesia (now Zimbabwe) were pioneers in adopting SAS techniques outside the United Kingdom, the New Zealanders together with the Long Range Desert Group were involved in special operations in the Western Desert from the very beginning.

In 1954, the New Zealand Government approved the formation of an independent Special Air Service Squadron to operate with 22 SAS in Malaya. Out of 800 volunteers, only 138 were selected for further training. By the time the new squadron moved to Malaya for parachute training at the end of 1955, another 49 had been replaced by more suitable men. Maoris comprised one-third of the team that finally went to Malaya. At this time, the SAS was normally in the jungle for thirteen weeks, time enough to achieve an understanding with the uncommitted aborigines; time enough also to make fighting contact with the Communists who were intimidating them.

After five weeks' reconnaissance in Pahang, the New Zealand Squadron took part in two standard operations to hunt down the Communist team led by Ah Ming. This team, consisting of eleven men, had for years dominated the Fort Brooke area on the Perak—Kelantan border and the aborigines living there. During those two operations, eight terrorists, including Ah Ming and his second-in-command, were killed and two terrorists wounded. One aborigine who had joined the terrorists was captured. Approximately 1,200 aborigines were re-grouped into two main areas. The Squadron lost one lead scout — who was mortally wounded when the enemy sprang an ambush — and one other soldier. The New Zealand Squadron was in Malaya for just over 24 months. Of that time, the unit's fighting men — a total of 90 — spent seventeen months in the jungle. The last three 13-week operations were in 400 square miles of rugged mountain in Negri Sembilan, where terrorist operations were conducted with sophistication by Li-Hak-Chi. As a result of the New Zealanders' penetration of the area, eight terrorists including Li-Hak-Chi himself were killed, two wounded and nine surrendered. The Squadron returned to New Zealand in December 1957, where it was then disbanded.

In 1959, however, Lieutenant-Colonel F. Rennie, MBE — commander of the Squadron on its formation and now Director of Infantry and Training at Army Headquarters — persuaded the Army that an SAS nucleus was necessary, and a troop was selected towards the end of the year. This later grew to squadron strength once more. In 1962, a detachment of 30 men commanded by Major M. N. Velvin carried out specialist duties in Thailand alongside American Special Forces. Such were the links with the Americans that, for a time, the unit title was changed to 1 Ranger Squadron, NZSAS.

During Confrontation with Indonesia in 1965 and 1966 four detachments from the Squadron served in Borneo, carrying out reconnaissance and ambush missions. Two years later, in November 1968, 4 Troops of the New Zealand SAS was deployed to South Vietman under the operational control of an Australian SAS squadron at Nui Dat. With a total strength of one officer and 25 men, the troop provided five-man patrols for long-range reconnaissance and ambush missions. Each soldier served twelve months in Vietnam until the troop was withdrawn in February 1971.

Since then, the Squadron has participated in excercises in Brunei, Malaysia, the Philippines, Singapore, Fiji and Australia. It has also played host in New Zealand to Allied special forces training in New Zealand. The description '1 Ranger Squadron' had also disappeared. Since April 1978 the unit has been redesignated as 1 NZSAS Squadron. Its men wear the red beret of British airborne forces, and the SAS winged dagger.

▽349

349-352. In 1955, led by their Officer Commanding, Frank Rennie, MC, the original New Zealand SAS Squadron parades through Wellington before flying to Malaya (**349**). It was Rennie's personal intervention in December 1959 that led to the unit's resurrection after it had been officially disbanded at the end of the Malayan campaign. Before going into action, the New Zealanders carried out basic parachute training from RAF Changi, Singapore (**350**). This man carries on his chest a valise containing equipment which must be released from his harness before he lands. By 1956, the New Zealanders were getting to know the Malayan jungle rather well. This team (**351**), with the leading 'point' man armed with a pump action shotgun, moves

slowly, quietly and cautiously. In some situations, SAS soldiers found it necessary to move only ten minutes in every half-hour. The other twenty minutes were spent listening and waiting. Years later, the endurance required for such warfare was illustrated in the Queen Elizabeth II Army Memorial Museum at Waiouru. In this realistic tableau (**352**), the lead scout, with shotgun and machete-like pahang, is followed by the rest of a six-man patrol whose armoury includes the standard self-loading rifle.

△353

△354

△356 ▽359

△357 ▽360

353, 354. In May 1962, when the northern border of Thailand was threatened with guerrilla war, a contingent of 30 men from the New Zealand SAS Squadron served with US forces there. Here, some of the team board a Hastings transport on their way to a war that their presence helped to avert (**353**). While they were there, some of the New Zealanders played the role of an enemy guerrilla unit in training the indigenous Thai Army. The Thais did not think it entirely fair of the New Zealanders to hijack a lorry carrying their lunch, and then use the vehicle to infiltrate the Thais' position. Typical of the men who served in Thailand were these two (**354**), photographed as they were absorbed in reading letters from home. Unlike British SAS soldiers, they retain the red beret, and slings attached to their rifles.

355-358. The New Zealanders were in action again in 1964 alongside the British and Australian SAS regiments, in fighting the regular Indonesian Army in Borneo, which was now part of Malaysia. During the same year, the Governor General of New Zealand inspected the Squadron at its Papakura Camp. The Governor General, Sir Bernard Fergusson (**355**), knew something about guerrilla and jungle warfare himself: he was a Chindit veteran of the Second World War. The selection course at that time included a swim with boots, rifle and pack (**356**) followed by continuation training with one of the specialized troops. Here (**357**), a boat troop comes ashore near Auckland while others, in the same area, learn the techniques of a mobility troop (**358**). As a space-saving device, bergen rucksacks are slung outside the vehicle. How many were lost is not recorded.

359-361. Between 1964 and 1966, as Confrontation continued, so, just as relentlessly, did SAS selection and training. Here (**359**), candidates for selection have rucksacks weighed off by their colour sergeant. After the long marches of selection, basic parachute training (**360**) seems comparatively easy. More exotic things followed, as these troopers embarking on HMNZS *Rotoiti* discovered (**361**). The footwear is varied and the submachine-guns are carried with magazines attached. The naval officer of the watch, unused to such rum customers, scratches his chin thoughtfully.

△355

△358 ▽361

△362 ▽363

362-365. Today, the New Zealand SAS remains in touch not only with special forces technology, but in one department — free-fall parachuting — it appears to be one step ahead of the British regiments in the equipment it uses. In **362** a trooper makes a dive exit through the open bomb doors of an RNZAF Andover at 10,000ft above Whenuapai air base near Auckland in December 1981. The familiar bulk of the chest-mounted reserve parachute is missing. He carries a single altimeter on a special mounting and has space up front for ammunition pouches. Experienced civilian skydivers now use a back-mounted unitary container for both main and reserve canopies. The soldier in **363** has equipment very similar to that, and vividly tidier than the gear used by the British SAS (see page 111). But he still might have problems. With his rifle apparently sliding across the front of his left leg, he appears to have some difficulty in staying stable at 6,000ft, well after leaving the aircraft. At 2,000ft the soldier has pulled the ripcord handle (**364**). The pilot chute (extractor), with bridle cord attached to it, is riding clear out of the container, from which it will draw the main canopy. The bergen ruck-sack is attached in the traditional position, beneath the main container. The rifle is now riding in the correct position, free of the soldier's leg. The reserve, following the pattern of civilian equipment, is in the upper part of the container, between the shoulder blades. It will be deployed only if there is a serious malfunction by the main canopy. Happily, this does not happen, though the type of canopy is not revealed by the last photograph in the sequence (**365**). It seems likely that the parachute gear used here is of American origin.

△364 ▽365

△366

367 ▷

366. The New Zealand SAS, unlike the British, took part in the war in Vietnam. New Zealanders, along with Australians, passed on some of the lessons of that war to other Allied forces, including those of Britain, at the Jungle Warfare School in Malaysia. From November 1968 until February 1971, the New Zealand Squadron's 4 Troop — one captain and 25 other ranks — was making deep reconnaissance penetration into Vietcong territory and ambushing enemy supply lines. The men involved served a twelve-month tour before returning to New Zealand. This soldier, photographed in Vietnam in 1970, was one of them. He is armed with an Armalite 5.56mm M16A1 selective fire rifle equipped with a grenade launcher.

367. Like all SAS units, the New Zealand Squadron produces some characters who are larger than life. One of them is Major Albert ('Alby') Kiwi, a Ngapuhi Maori who is as well known among high altitude military parachutists in Britain as he is in Australia and New Zealand. In 1978, Kiwi, a quietly spoken but determined man, ran the 1,380 miles from Bluff, at New Zealand's southern extremity, to Cape Reinga at the other end of the country to raise funds for the military museum at Waiouru. His journey took 31 days, an average of 4.7mph. Kiwi did not travel the entire distance alone. His Labrador-cross, 'Freefall' went with him for 600 miles (as well as 500 miles in training). During the last phase of the journey, the dog wore specially fitted yellow leather boots to protect his paws. Kiwi's achievement was characteristic of SAS feats of endurance. Others include the Everest ascent by Stokes and Lane, the Atlantic row by Trooper T. ('Moby') McLean and the Fiennes expedition. The Maori's comments afterwards were also in keeping with much SAS thinking elsewhere: 'We're a small, modest army, but a proud one. . . . I was a man with a mission and I have accomplished it.'

The Falklands
A synthesis of things past

It could have been another Gallipoli, an opposed landing on a defended beachhead thousands of miles from home, ending in disaster. Instead, the Falklands campaign was a triumph of British arms. That the vulnerable landing force was not obliged to march to its death through the cold, swirling waters of San Carlos anchorage was due to the special forces Britain had already put ashore: the SAS, the SBS, and the specialist aircrew (most of them Royal Navy men) who carried them. This success called upon virtually every technique in the SAS/SBS armoury: appallingly hazardous amphibious work by divers and Boat Troop specialists; 'wet drops' by parachute into the sea; nocturnal helicopter operations; prolonged periods of concealment in freezing, wet conditions; uniquely hard endurance marches on foot and ski; above all, a mastery of long distance communications behind enemy lines.

Hostilities began in March 1982 with the arrival of Argentinian 'scrap metal merchants' on South Georgia and military occupation soon afterward. The invasion of the Falklands, 800 miles away, followed on 2 April. On 21 April, the first SAS reconnaissance party of fifteen men went ashore by helicopter on South Georgia, an island that is nearer to Antarctica than it is to the Falklands. In grim, Antarctic weather this team was placed on the 1,800ft Fortuna Glacier, some miles inland, overlooking the administrative capital of Grytviken. The town, an ancient whaling port, was now held by an Argentine garrison of 150 in spite of the fact that South Georgia was discovered and claimed for Britain by Captain Cook in 1775.

The weather defeated this first SAS party. Winds exceeding 100mph swept away their bivouac tents and a blizzard made observation impossible. Left there much longer they would die of exposure. Two Wessex helicopters sent to recover the men crashed in 'white-out' conditions after having taken the SAS soldiers on board. Unabashed by this, Lieutenant-Commander Ian Stanley flew seven sorties in two days in a third Wessex in his efforts to rescue the soldiers and the crews of the crashed aircraft now stranded with them. When he finally succeeded, Stanley's aircraft carried a fearsome overload of seventeen passengers. He was awarded a DSO.

Meanwhile, aboard their base, the destroyer *Antrim* — known in the trade as 'the grey ghost' because 'no-one knows where the hell we are' — the SAS plotted another way into the island. Their commander sent a second fifteen-man team ashore in five inflatable Gemini rubber boats powered by unreliable outboard engines. Their objective was Grass Island, within sight of Grytviken. Of the five boats, only three reached their objective. Two were swept away after their engines failed. The tiny vessels drifted helplessly in the dark before a strong wind, on a heavy swell. The following morning a radio beacon from one of these craft enabled a search helicopter to locate it and rescue the men on board. The second missing party was not found so easily. The drifting Gemini was making good progress towards Antarctica when it was blown close to a remote South Georgia peninsular which was the last landfall for thousands of miles. The men waded ashore. Then, to avoid compromising the operation by sending a radio signal for help, they put their survival training into practice for five days. They signalled and were rescued only after the final surrender of Argentine forces in the area.

The nine SAS men who did reach Grass Island were able to keep the enemy under close scrutiny and report that he seemed lethargic and careless. A group of Royal Marine SBS men successfully infiltrated farther south, on the main island, and reached the same conclusion.

The land forces which recaptured South Georgia were technically under the command of a Royal Marine officer, Major Guy Sheridan, whose rank equates with the Army's lieutenant-colonel. But such are the fortunes of war that when the opportunity came to seize Grytviken, Sheridan's main commando force was involved elsewhere in a hazardous 'RAS', or resupply-at-sea operation. In the event, reoccupation followed the discovery of the Argentine submarine *Santa Fe* by Royal Navy helicopter pilots, including Ian Stanley. The helicopters hit the vessel as it approached Grytviken on the surface with a depth charge, anti-ship missiles and machine-gun fire. Crippled, the vessel ran aground in the harbour. To the amazement of the helicopter crew, forty Argentine marines — reinforcements for the enemy garrison — were seen to flee ashore with the submariners.

From *Antrim*'s bridge the SAS squadron commander, a major, watched what was happening with quickening interest. His instincts suggested that at this moment of confusion ashore, the time was ripe for an assault. *Antrim*'s skipper, Captain Brian Young — who was in overall command of the island's recapture — agreed. One SAS party already ashore had with it a Royal Artillery officer to act as an expert spotter for the *Antrim*'s 4.5in guns. Later, aboard *Invincible*, this officer told correspondents: 'I commenced a bombardment of the shore but was not allowed to engage targets closer than 800 yards from the enemy position. I was very careful not to do that because at that stage we merely wished to demonstrate superior firepower and to clear the area that would be required to be used by our own troops.'

Under cover of this bombardment, the SAS commander ordered an instant attack by the thirty men at his disposal and they swept ashore by helicopter, landing three miles from Grytviken. As they moved menacingly forward on the settlement, the Argentines held their fire, confident that the British would die at any second. But as the SAS stormed on, the minefield they were supposed to die in, lay quiescent. There was no further resistance and the Argentine commander, Captain Alfredo Astiz, ordered a surrender. As the SAS ran up the Union Jack, an Argentine officer lamented: 'You have just run through a minefield.' According to the Gunner officer quoted above, 'The surrender was in fact before the ground forces came within small arms range. The enemy never fired a shot. I think the naval gunfire must have had a very demoralizing effect on the enemy, especially since the fire was brought down around them in a controlled

△368

△369

pattern, so they obviously were able to observe that we could have hit them if we wanted to.' Royal Marine Commandos followed the SAS ashore at Grytviken and next day seized Leith, where yet another SAS reconnaissance party was already active.

The recovery of South Georgia was of such significance that the Government, in awarding a DSO to Captain Brian Young, RN, emphasized: 'The importance of this operation to the overall strategy of re-establishing British administration in the Falkland Islands and its dependencies cannot be overstated . . .' It boosted public confidence in the Government's forceful response to aggression at a critical time. It also restored Britain's stake in the strategically important British Antarctic Territory, to parts of which Argentina had long laid claim. It demonstrated, yet again, the capacity of a handful of well-trained, adventurous men to bring down tons of high explosive, with terrible precision, from land or sea-based artillery, or from the air. Ultimately, the physical reoccupation of South Georgia was the result of inspired timing and opportunism by the SAS, without casualties. Never was the Regiment's motto — 'Who Dares Wins' — more completely vindicated.

Grytviken was retaken on 25 April. The first SAS landing on the Falklands followed only six days later on 1 May, almost three weeks before the main landing at San Carlos by the Parachute Regiment and Royal Marines. By now, additional SAS men were joining the operation from widely scattered points around the globe, taking daunting short cuts in the process.

Initially, the job of both SAS and SBS teams in the Falklands was reconnaissance. Over the horizon the task force commander, Rear Admiral 'Sandy' Woodward, could not afford a single serious error in landing his force. Failure to get it right first time would turn round political opinion in Britain, the EEC and the UN Security Council. He needed to know which areas of the Falklands were well defended and where the gaps were. Which offered deep water anchorages? Were enemy artillery or locally-based aircraft a threat to the landing? Were there minefields? To be sure, the information at Woodward's disposal included American satellite data, but this was limited in two ways. Dense cloud cover most of the time meant that satellite photographs would show little more than the tops of clouds. And, as the fleet closed towards the shore, the time taken to retrieve and process satellite information, and then feed it to the fleet, was so great as to make that information stale and value-less. As the questions multiplied in *Invincible*'s operations centre, it became luminously obvious that the only safe answer was a consistent flow of information from teams of soldiers on the ground. The responsibility carried by the

men who performed this delicate task, even by SAS standards, was extraordinary. A total of 5,000 troops was to be put ashore in closely-packed landing craft which — as the grievous losses resulting from the subsequent bombing of *Sir Galahad* demonstrated — were sitting ducks for enemy guns and aircraft.

In general, it is true to say that the SBS commandos, brave and skilled as they are, are fewer in number than the SAS and have less recent combat experience. In spite of this they performed excellently in carrying out their 'sneaky-beaky' exploration of coastal waters and beaches. To them must go the credit for discovering that San Carlos, a daring choice for the main landing of 21 May, was virtually undefended by the Argentines.

It was the SAS, however, which performed its traditional function of worming its way in among enemy positions to watch, listen, count and report back to the task force. For the Regiment, this was largely a helicopter war. In driving rain and sleet and almost total darkness, Royal Navy pilots delivered them time and again to isolated parts of East and West Falkland, flying low all the way. Each four-man team abseiled from the aircraft into the squelching bog to begin a long, nerve-racking march to the target area with no hope of aid if things went wrong. Once in position, the teams were staked out, immobile, in the freezing peat for up to 48 hours at a time.

Each day, every team would snap back to its base an accelerated, coded message in radio morse if only to report that it was still on station and active. According to US reports, some teams also carried American radios which linked them, via US military satellites, direct with London. Anxiety for one team grew when two days passed without a signal. Finally, on the third day, the team came on the air to explain that it had been in the centre of an Argentine position. Even a few seconds of morse could have betrayed its presence. Another team, equipped like the rest with a fourteen-day supply of rations had to make even that meagre, dehydrated diet last 26 days. One of them compared the immobility and lack of food to a particularly hard stake-out on the Irish border, except that this was just as wet, and much colder. The prolonged stress involved was akin to the cross-border operations in Borneo. The 'trench foot' most of them contracted was reminiscent of Flanders.

At the end of such a patrol the men would crawl and then march to the helicopter rendezvous to be extracted. As the machine swept in over the moorland, its engine noise dissipated by relentless wind, the SAS men cautiously signalled it in with Vordic torches, which give only a thin beam of light upward. The machines rarely landed. Each man, still burdened with rucksack and rifle, squelched to the point

where a rope was lowered for him to climb a few feet into the unaccustomed warmth of the helicopter while his comrades, weapons ready, covered him.

With the approach of D-Day, 21 May, the SAS took on an offensive, raiding role as well as that of reconnaissance. With at least two squadrons deployed, one was given the task of attacking the enemy, the other, that of spying on him. It is a fine point which task was the more exacting. Raids performed several functions. They removed possible threats to the task force. They sowed doubt in the enemy's mind about where the main landing would be. Ultimately, they fooled the Argentine garrison into assuming that this landing, when it did finally take place, was just another in-and-out assault.

In the most spectacular of these raids an SAS squadron destroyed eleven Pucara ground attack aircraft on Pebble Island airstrip on the night of 14/15 May. The same squadron had liberated South Georgia. It was an eventful ride. Under cover of darkness on 11 May, an SAS reconnaissance and reception party was first put ashore by helicopter on a bleak, rocky peninsular of West Falkland opposite the 800-yard Tamar Pass lying between West Falkland and Pebble Island. The men had to cross this stretch of dangerous tidal water by canoe. After 24 hours they were still waiting for the weather to ease and at last they slipped into the sea and paddled across.

After sinking these vessels to conceal their presence the team marched to high ground and established observation posts overlooking the Argentine dug-outs and airstrip. The following night, their third on hostile territory, they reached the rendezvous with the main force in the nick of time, identifying the landing zone for helicopters bringing in 45 SAS raiders from the same squadron. The helicopters arrived late and there was now a mere 30 minutes of darkness left within which to operate safely.

A short march brought them to the airstrip, at which point all hell was let loose. A Royal Navy gunnery expert with the SAS men directed 4.5 inch naval artillery shells onto the positions occupied by Argentinians around the airfield. Meanwhile, in the darkness, twelve four-man SAS teams attached explosive firebombs to the aircraft, aircraft which could have created havoc among the main force when it landed ten days later at nearby San Carlos. Fuel and ammunition dumps were also attacked and any Argentine soldier unwise enough to try to intercept the raiders — the first was an officer — was cut down by machine-gun fire. As the raiders withdrew to the helicopter rendezvous the first aircraft exploded into the night sky, followed by an enormous blast as fuel stores went up. All those involved in this raid returned safely, although two had suffered minor

368. A scene that shocked Britain and her allies: Royal Marine Commandos of the tiny Falklands garrison are forced to lie prostrate in the road after the Governor, Rex Hunt, had ordered them to surrender to invading Argentine forces — by whom they were outnumbered ten to one — on 2 April 1982. Standing over the commandos are Argentine special forces men from Unit 602, trained by US special forces. A day or so later, a British marine, on his way home by way of Uruguay, promised, 'We'll be back.'
369-371. Argentine dedication to possession of the 'Malvinas' extended extravagantly 800 miles beyond the Falklands to South Georgia, on the fringe of Antarctica. South Georgia, then uninhabited, was possessed for Britain by Captain Cook in 1775. Argentine interest in the territory dates from 1927. On 2 April 1982, the invaders were led by a naval officer who doubled as a government undercover agent and torturer, Captain Alfredo Astiz, identified here (**369**) parading at Grytviken after the invasion and, in **370** (foreground, second from the left), with a civilian. Was this one of the 'scrap metal merchants' whose illegal entry into South Georgia some weeks before had artificially detonated the Falklands conflict? And was he working throughout for the 'dirty tricks' specialist Astiz? It is one explanation for putting such a politically sophisticated — and compromised — officer into South Georgia and possible control of Britain's Antarctic Territory. By the time Astiz surrendered to the SAS and signed a formal surrender document on board HMS *Plymouth* (**371**) he had grown a beard. Astiz was brought to Britain to answer questions raised by the Swedish and French Governments about some of their citizens who had vanished while in the custody of Astiz. Exercising his rights under the Geneva Convention, he declined to answer. So the disappearance of a seventeen-year-old Swedish girl and two aged French nuns remains a mystery. Astiz was not interrogated by the SAS in South Georgia or in Britain. He was flown to Montevideo, in neutral Uruguay, where he disappeared. The Argentine Government made no complaint about this. Their citizens often disappear.

gunshot wounds in a whirlwind of bullets which knocked them down.

It was peculiarly tragic, as well as ironic, that eighteen of their number were to be killed a few days later in a helicopter crash caused not by enemy action but — it is the best guess — a bird strike. As part of the preparations for D-Day the men had attended a briefing aboard one of the task force carriers and were now on their way back to the assault ship *Intrepid* to pass on the briefing to others. Their Sea King helicopter carried a crew of four and 26 passengers, compensating for the larger-than-usual number of people with a reduced fuel load for the short journey. The departure from the carrier's heaving deck was uneventful. The Sea King then circled the ship, traversed a short stretch of water towards *Intrepid* and was starting its descent when the crew heard two loud reports from the engine. There was then a catastrophic loss of power and the helicopter dived 300ft into the sea, rolling as it did so. Because it struck the water at an angle, it was rapidly engulfed. Buoyancy bags, which might have kept the Sea King afloat had it settled evenly on the water, were of little help in this situation. Nine men survived, including one of the two who had been wounded on Pebble Island. Within seconds the big machine filled with water and disappeared. Floating debris left on the surface included a large quantity of sea-bird feathers, which amateur ornithologists in the task force identified as those of an albatross.

The SAS soldiers who died were: W.O. II Lawrence Gallagher, BEM; W.O. II Malcolm Atkinson; Staff Sergeant Patrick O'Connor; Sergeant Philip Currass, QGM; Sergeant Sid Davidson; Sergeant John Arthy; Sergeant William Hughes; Corporal Paul Bunker; Corporal William Begley; Corporal William Hatton, QGM; Corporal Philip Jones; Corporal John Newton; Corporal Michael McHugh; Corporal Stephen Sykes; Corporal Edward Walpole; Corporal Robert Burns; Corporal Douglas MacCormack; Lance Corporal Paul Lightfoot; Trooper Raymond Armstrong. Several of those drowned, including Currass, Davidson, 'Lofty' Arthy and 'Paddy' Armstrong, had survived both the Fortuna Glacier and Pebble Island operations. W.O. II Gallagher had carried the Union Jack ashore at Grytviken in his battle smock and hoisted it over South Georgia after that territory was retaken. Two others lost in the Sea King were Flight Lieutenant Garth Hawkins, an RAF specialist attached to the SAS, and Corporal Michael Love, Royal Marines. The casualty toll was greater than anything the Regiment had suffered in a single episode since the Second World War. One of the survivors, already nicknamed 'Splash' because of his experience of unpremeditated helicopter descents into the sea, added three more such crashes to his record during the Falklands campaign.

The Sea King was lost just 24 hours before the main British landing at San Carlos. As this was about to begin, 40 SAS soldiers from the combat squadron which had taken Grytviken and raided Pebble Island were making a forced march towards the heavily defended Argentine positions at Darwin and Goose Green, south of the main beachhead. It was now known that a small force of Argentinians had been moved forward to Fanning Head, overlooking San Carlos anchorage, and that the main threat would come from the garrison at Goose Green.

The Fanning Head group was attacked by men of the SBS. The group surrendered or fled, but not before it had shot down a British helicopter. But from San Carlos to Darwin is about twenty miles as the crow flies, and on foot through peat bog, in the dark, it is much farther. The SAS raiders' job was to fool the Argentine garrison into believing that moving forward, in the darkness, there was at least a battalion of 600 men or more. So what was required was a lot of firepower and much noise from teams numbering no more than a dozen or so. This in turn meant that the SAS soldiers had to carry a powerful supply of mortars, machine-guns and a cornucopia of ammunition. The orders were, Noise; Firepower; No Close Engagement. The march itself took twenty hours and each man carried 80lb. It was described to reporter Max Hastings by one of those involved as 'The toughest hike I've ever done with the SAS.' This raid, like so many others, was dramatically successful. As the SAS mortar bombs and machine-gun bullets whistled upon them out of the darkness, the Argentinians had no idea that they outnumbered their attackers by forty-to-one. Nor did they care to try to find out. As the SAS withdrew they shot down a Pucara with a Blowpipe SAM missile.

With the main landing accomplished at San Carlos, the enemy concentration at Goose Green was conquered by 2 Parachute Regiment in a memorable action during which the Commanding Officer, Lieutenant-Colonel H. Jones, was killed leading a platoon assault. (Subsequently, military men confidently predicted that his action would be recognized with a posthumous VC.) Meanwhile, 3 Para and a Royal Marine Commando made an almost unopposed advance along the northern edge of East Falkland.

372, 373. Above the ancient whaling port of Grytviken, sheer mountains scarred with windswept glaciers were the first, inhospitable landfall for British forces reoccupying territory seized by Argentina. Royal Navy helicopters flying 1,800ft above sea level in gale force blizzards put the first fifteen-man SAS reconnaissance team on to Fortuna Glacier, overlooking Grytviken. Even on rare days of clear weather, these South Georgia mountains are forbidding. As snow drives in over the same area (**372**), the pilot of this British helicopter on a special mission knows that at any second he will be flying totally blind, without a horizon. Efforts to recover the SAS team when their frail bivouacs were destroyed

◁**372**

The mountains between these two thrusts were an essential pivot from which they could be co-ordinated. Without that pivot, both British forces could be potentially out-flanked, cut off and driven into the sea. The task of establishing that pivot, on Mount Kent, was given to the SAS. The same squadron that had been in continuous offensive operations since Grytviken, and which had lost some of its best men in the Sea King crash, was once again in the front line, and beyond, foraging far ahead of the big battalions and operating at night.

Just as in the first days of the Italian campaign and the last months of the war in North-West Europe, the SAS was now being used as a forward reconnaissance screen rather than the job for which it was created. Characteristically, it was handling this dangerous task with panache. After one encounter on Mount Kent an SAS soldier crisply reported: 'Every time we get near an "Argy" patrol, they leg it. We ran into one the other night though . . . Took two, wounded two, killed three.' The seizure of Mount Kent, a windswept peak of 1,500ft dominating the approaches to Port Stanley, was accomplished by the SAS after a daring night approach in helicopters. After some confused fighting in the darkness, the squadron dug in, World War II-style and held the position until it was relieved by a somewhat larger force of Royal Marine Commandos.

For the rest of the campaign, SAS tactics followed this successful formula. Night reconnaissance patrols found the soft spots in the Argentine defences which were then exploited by the Paras and Commandos. The noose was tightening on the beleaguered Port Stanley garrison. But one potential mission remained for the SAS, one of the most delicate it had yet undertaken. This was to identify and, if possible, rescue the 600 Falkland Island civilians held hostage in the capital. In the event, mediation by the International Red Cross was intended to create a neutral zone around the Cathedral where the civilians would be safe. In turn, this scheme was overtaken by the dramatic collapse and surrender of the Argentinians as the British task force dominated the high ground immediately around the capital.

The South Atlantic campaign was to have momentous implications for Britain's defence policy. The exclusive attention of Whitehall to European defence in the years preceding 1982 came into question, in Whitehall. For the SAS, which had always contrived to produce strategic results out of all proportion to its numbers in the Gulf and elsewhere in the Third World (places just as important as Europe), this was good news.

One immediate and more tangible result of the campaign was that the SAS had demonstrated that it had learned much and — in spite of an apparent carelessness about its own past and traditions — it had forgotten nothing about the lessons of the Second World War. The Falklands campaign was a synthesis of the offensive raiding traditions of Stirling's desert SAS and the painfully acquired experience of post-war campaigns in which minimum force, precise intelligence, persuasion and the manipulation of perceptions — enemy and civilian alike — became as important as military muscle.

In a world changed beyond recognition by modern communications, limited wars of this sort are no longer fought in a vacuum. The political and public relations impact of military success or failure, or victory linked to unnecessary slaughter, is instant and worldwide. For the entire task force, military victory with minimum loss of life on both sides was essential if the victory was to be 'real' and enjoy international approval. In this, as in so many areas, the SAS were the pioneers.

What might be described, after the Falklands, as the 'SAS synthesis', was historically inevitable. Warfare might have occurred on this scale, and in this style, in Europe or Scandinavia at any time over the past thirty years. That it should occur 8,000 miles away in the Falklands should not diminish the significance of what has happened. The 'SAS synthesis' — high technology weaponry combined with 'low intensity' strategy — is greater than the sum of its parts. When it is applied to an entire military campaign, as it was in the Falklands, a new style of warfare has started to evolve.

by the blizzard merely made matters worse. Two Wessex helicopters sent to the rescue became victims also and crashed during a 'white-out' in what was now enemy territory. The result of that mishap was surveyed (**373**) in characteristically foul weather by an SAS ski patrol after the liberation of South Georgia. Only the repeated heroism of another Royal Navy pilot, Lieutenant-Commander Ian Stanley, saved the men. Captain Scott, writing his Antarctic diary just before he died of exposure there in 1912, commented: 'God! This is an awful place . . . .' The SAS team, and the aircrew stranded with it, reached the same conclusion and almost met the same fate as Scott's party.

△374

△377 ▽378

△375

379 ▷

△376

△380 ▽381

374-376. When the Argentine submarine *Santa Fe* approached Grytviken on the surface, carrying reinforcements for the Astiz garrison there, Royal Navy helicopters swooped down and hit it with missiles. The crippled vessel ran aground in the whaling berth (**374**). There was panic among the Argentines . . . a good moment, an SAS squadron commander suggested, to seize the place. Backed up by a carefully ranged naval bombardment orchestrated from a gunnery officer already ashore with the SAS, the squadron landed by helicopter. It was the first of a series of intensive operations by the same squadron that would take in the raids on Pebble Island and Goose Green and much else. With South Georgia liberated, it was an SAS Warrant Officer, Sergeant-Major Lawrence Gallagher, BEM (left, **375**), who proudly hoisted the Union Jack, which he had carried ashore inside his battle smock. Argentine soldiers, not too unhappy to be out of the war, were rounded up (**376**) by the SAS and Royal Marines.

377-381. The essential preliminary to recapturing the Falkland Islands was the special forces' intelligence gathering operation. The SBS, seen training in these pictures (**377-379**) explored the coastline of East Falkland and made the momentous discovery that San Carlos deep-water anchorage — chosen as the main British beachhead — was virtually undefended. Both SBS and SAS men found shelter during these operations in many of the islands' caves. Here (**380**) a Royal Marine Commando peers out of his 'nest' in the Falklands, for which the men sometimes had to compete with penguins. The SAS squadron given the task of spying on the enemy had to penetrate deep inland, always moving under cover of darkness. The Argentinians, who themselves practised concealment, as in these scenes photographed during the occupation (**381**), never detected such patrols. Criticism that British intelligence had underestimated the number of enemy at Goose Green and Port Stanley, itself underestimated the problem of obtaining precise information about numbers. It was enough to know which areas were defended in force. As one reconnaissance expert put it: 'We could hardly walk up to them and call the roll.'

△382 ▽383 ▽384

▽385 386▷

382, 383. Pebble Island, off the north coast of West Falkland, as it was after the Argentine invasion but before the SAS raid of 16 May, which destroyed its military value to the enemy. In this montage photograph (**382**), a pair of Argentine Pucara ground attack aircraft are seen above the airstrip at Pebble. The perspective is that of the SAS reconnaissance force as it moved along the high ground overlooking the grass airstrip (foreground) and Pebble Island settlement on the coastline (background), with the difference that the SAS saw it by night. The Pucaras could have wrought devastation among the landing craft at nearby San Carlos a few days later and it was imperative that they be destroyed. But the naval barrage had to avoid the civilian settlement. While the SAS raiding party — drawn from the same squadron that had recaptured Grytviken — planted bombs on the aircraft, a gunnery expert brought in with the SAS directed the shell fire. The first people to learn that this was an SAS attack were Argentine soldiers in the Falklands. A Defence Ministry broadcasting station on Ascension Island, Radio Atlantico del Sud, used a smooth, sibilant female voice to tell the Argentinians, in Spanish, that the SAS had used twelve four-man teams for the raid. The SAS, explained Radio Atlantico, specialized in clandestine operations. 'They are very highly trained soldiers, the best in the world. They are all volunteers, but the standards are so high that only one in fifty is selected.' This did not improve the morale of gloomy conscripts. The announcement was the first official confirmation that the Regiment was in action in the Falklands, although there had been much press speculation — most of it ill-informed — about SAS activities there. Prisoners were also taken during special forces' raids on West Falkland, as a useful source of information. In **383** two of them are interviewed aboard a task force vessel by a Royal Navy interpreter. In one such raid, Captain Gavin Hamilton, aged 29, an SAS troop commander, was killed.

384, 385. One of the most enigmatic reconnaissance missions of the war concerned a Royal Navy Sea King helicopter that was found (**385**) on 20 May, burned out and abandoned ten miles south of Punta Arenas in neutral Chile, far from the main British task force but remarkably close to neighbouring Argentine air bases. From one of these bases the deadly combination of Super Etendard aircraft equipped with Exocet sea-skimming missiles continued to threaten the British fleet after the destruction of HMS *Sheffield* on 4 May. The helicopter crew, having destroyed their aircraft, hid in the countryside for a week in the belief, they said, that they were in Argentina. The episode inevitably sparked off speculation about a clandestine special forces operation . . . to destroy the Etendards; to set up secret radar facilities from which Argentine attacks could be monitored from the moment they took off; to obtain data useful for a Vulcan bomber raid on the Argentine mainland; to pick up British secret agents . . . and so on. If any of these explanations were true, there was no confirmation from British sources. All that was plain, from the wreckage and the survivors, was that something had gone very wrong. At a ten-minute press conference in Chile (**384**), the helicopter crew — Lieutenant Alan Bennett (left), Petty Officer Peter Imrie and Lieutenant Richard Hutchings (pilot) — threw little light on the affair. Hutchings said, 'We were on sea patrol when we experienced engine failure due to adverse weather. It was not possible to return to our ship in these conditions. We therefore took refuge in the nearest neutral country.' After Port Stanley fell, an inaccurate report in the London *Sunday Times* suggested that seven SAS soldiers were secretly held captive in Argentina after an operation at Rio Gallegos military base in southern Argentina. The report — published despite denials in London and Buenos Aires — caused much distress to the widows of SAS men lost in a Sea King helicopter accident (see next caption): some of the bereaved were falsely led to hope that their men might be alive after all.

386. For the SAS NCOs who had already seized South Georgia and raided Pebble Island, the Sea King helicopter trip to their assault ship after an operational briefing aboard one of the task force carriers on 20 May should have been a routine transfer. Their minds were still turning over the implications of the briefing: a prolonged march with heavy equipment, through a peat bog, with a battle at the end of it to keep a powerful Argentine force contained at Goose Green during the British landing at San Carlos. It was dusk and the conditions outside were as turbulent as ever. No lights were permitted. The Sea King was packed with passengers — theoretically overloaded — but the additional weight was no risk. The pilot, with only a short flight, had reduced his fuel load. The Sea King, in service with the Royal Navy and Royal Marines since 1969, was a familiar and reliable work-horse in northern Norway or (as in this picture of Marines rehearsing for the Falklands) on Dartmoor. At 300ft, as the machine started its descent, those on board heard a thump, then a second report, from the engine. The Sea King dipped, then dived. Within four seconds it was in the water. Some men were killed or knocked unconscious in the initial impact. But somehow, through an open door or a hole in the fuselage, nine men who were not restrained by safety belts scrambled out of the upturned, sinking craft and came splashing to the surface of the icy water. They were the only survivors. Rescuers noted bird feathers among the debris still floating as the helicopter vanished. If, as seems likely, the cause of the disaster was a bird strike, two birds might have been responsible. The black browed albatross, with an 8ft wing span, might have been attracted to the Sea King as a result of fatal curiosity. More probably it was a giant petrel. Flocks of these will routinely follow a ship in the South Atlantic to feed off rubbish thrown overboard. An entire fleet would attract more petrels than usual. Either an albatross or a petrel trapped in the helicopter engine's inlet manifold could have caused engine failure. Of the nine SAS survivors, one had been wounded only four days before at Pebble Island.

△387

U N C L A S S I F I E D
SIC 19F
THE FOL IS THE TEXT OF A MSG FROM 317.1 PASSED VIA HEREFORD TO
ADDRESSEES ABOVE. MSG BEGINS.
HQ LFFI PORT STANLEY. IN PORT STANLEY AT 9 O!CLOCK PM FALKLAND
ISLANDS TIME TONIGHT THE 14 JUNE 1982, MAJOR GENERAL MENENDES
SURRENDERED TO ME ALL THE ARGENTINE ARMED FORCES IN EAST AND WEST
FALKLAND, TOGETHER WITH THEIR IMPEDIMENTA. ARRANGEMENTS ARE IN
HAND TO ASSEMBLE THE MEN FOR RETURN TO ARGENTINA, TO GATHER IN
THEIR ARMS AND EQUIPMENT, AND TO MARK AND MAKE SAFE THEIR MUNITIONS.
THE FALKLAND ISLANDS ARE ONCE MORE UNDER THE GOVERNMENT DESIRED

PAGE 2 RBDTWM 002 UNCLAS
BY THEIR INHABITANTS.
GOD SAVE THE QUEEN.
SIGNED JJ MOORE.
MSG ENDS
BT

▽388 △389

387, 388. Within 24 hours of the Sea King disaster the main British task force of 5,000 Royal Marines and Parachute Regiment soldiers was launched ashore unmolested (**387**) at San Carlos on 21 May. For the Argentinians, it was the beginning of the end, although — with their customary, unreal optimism — they did not believe an army could march with food and ammunition across a trackless moor, sixty miles or more, to attack Port Stanley. Initially, they were persuaded that this was yet another special forces' raid, a suspicion cultivated by the SAS night attack, coinciding with the main landing, on the Argentine main garrison at Goose Green. For the SAS squadron involved in undercover, 'keeni-meeni' reconnaissance, it was a time of intense activity. It had started with the first air attack on Port Stanley on 1 May. Later, as the battle for Goose Green developed, British reports from Argentina spoke of some very strange events which, if true, could only be the work of special forces. 'We thought we were fighting men from another galaxy', said one Argentine officer. Why? Because of mysterious interruptions in Argentine ground communications, disrupted radar and, worst of all, because Argentine detection systems 'saw British troops where there weren't any. Our troops were drawn out to chase ghosts. It was very unnerving.' Other deep penetration patrols used the services of Falkland Islands militiamen. One of these told reporter Alastair McQueen: 'We have been so close to those old Argies that we could see them in the moonlight and hear them talking. I could understand what they were saying. I have had the odd Argy in my sights but I couldn't shoot because it would have given our position away. So they had to stay alive.' For the reconnaissance teams, unlike the combat squads, there was no 'action' to relieve such tension. And from the time Mount Kent was occupied, SAS patrols penetrated Port Stanley itself. They identified the sites used by land-launched Exocet missiles. These were then destroyed by Harrier jets, naval gunfire or, if all else failed, on-the-spot sabotage. But one Exocet that survived, mounted on a lorry and moved to avoid the same fate, struck the destroyer *Glamorgan* during the final assault on the capital. The desolate terrain over which the SAS men flew, marched, and sometimes crawled, is illustrated in **388**: Two Sisters mountain, seen from Mount Kent, looking towards Port Stanley. **389-392.** The moment of surrender by General Menendez and his troops was signalled back to London by way of the SAS base at Hereford, as this message from Major-General Jeremy Moore to the British Government (**389**) reveals. This was appropriate. Preliminary negotiations with Menendez were conducted by Lieutenant-Colonel Mike Rose, QGM, then commanding 22 SAS. Hitherto all but concealed, the role of the SAS, SBS and their helicopter crews was a decisive factor in an astonishing military victory in which an outnumbered force, operating 8,000 miles from home without adequate air cover, regained the Falklands with the loss of only 250 British lives. Occasionally, the Argentinians surrendered singly (**391**), but more often in battalion strength (**390**). The man who led this folly, General Leopoldo Galtieri, like some twentieth century Don Quixote (**392**), rode into political obscurity. The world got the message, as it had done before, that Britain is rarely prepared for war, but, if it has to fight, it will fight to win.

△390

△391

△392

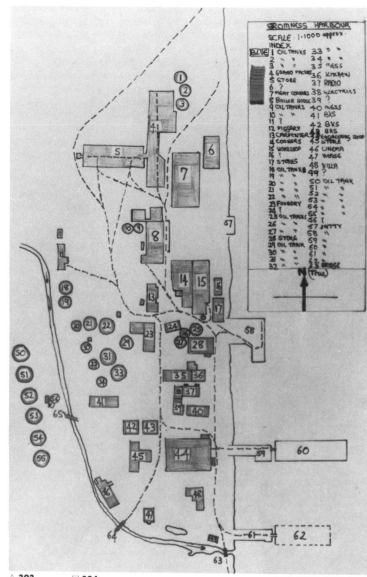

STROMNESS HARBOUR
SCALE 1:1000 approx.
INDEX
BLUE 1 OIL TANKS 33 "
2 " " 34 "
3 " " 35 MESS
4 GUANO FACT. 36 KITCHEN
5 STORE 37 RADIO
6 ? 38 ELECTRICS
7 BOAT CHARS 39 ?
8 BOILER HOUSE 40 MESS
9 OIL TANKS 41 BKS
10 " " 42 BKS
11 ? 43 BKS
12 PIGGERY 44 ENGINEERING SHOP
13 CARPENTER 45 STORE
14 COOKERS 46 CINEMA
15 WORKSHOP 47 HORSE
16 ? 48 VILLA
17 STORES 49 ?
18 OIL TANKS 50 OIL TANK
19 " 51 "
20 " " 52 "
21 " " 53 "
22 " " 54 "
23 FOUNDRY 55 "
24 OIL TANKS 56 ?
25 " " 57 JETTY
26 " " 58 "
27 STORE 59 "
28 " 60 "
29 OIL TANK 61 "
30 " 62 "
31 " 63 BRIDGE
32 "
N (True)

△ 393   ▽ 394

△ 395

△ 396   ▽ 397

△ **398** ▽ **399**

Almost a year after the Argentine surrender, photographs taken during the conflict were released to the author. Some of these augment this new Fontana edition of *This is the SAS*. On facing page and this page: **393:** SAS plan of Stromness prior to Fortuna Glacier operation. Operational detail was such that even the Piggery (no. 12 on plan) was identified. In **394** and inset picture men of D Squadron start their ill-fated journey to the glacier from Antrim. Photograph **373** records the result. After South Georgia came a series of cross-decking operations by helicopter over the angry, cold Atlantic as the SAS put reconnaissance and raiding parties into the occupied Falklands. In **395** men of D Squadron wait to fly by Sea King helicopter from Hermes. During one such flight a Sea King was lost with 20 SAS and attached personnel. In this photograph, faces are obscured for security reasons: the men concerned are still serving. The Sea King disaster occurred soon after the now famous Pebble Island raid. Here (**396**) an official reconnaissance picture shows some of the wreckage at the intersection of two runways. While D Squadron was making raids the men of G Squadron were silently 'grovelling in the peat' in hidden observation posts, watching the Argentines at close quarters. Movement to and from these OPs was by night, so the men slept by day on their way back to helicopter rendezvous. As photograph **397** reveals, they took it in turns to sleep in bivvy bags but slept with rifle in hand. When the Argentines surrendered at South Georgia and in the Falklands, they did so to SAS officers. In **398** a helicopter trailing white truce flag carries SAS Commanding Officer, Lieutenant-Colonel H.M. Rose, DSO, QGM, to meet Argentine General Menendez in Port Stanley. After negotiating the surrender Rose was toasted by Argentine headquarters staff drinking Southern Comfort. Rose then hoisted the SAS Union Jack on Government House flagstaff before returning to Britain. But some men did not come home. Among them was Captain John Hamilton, who died heroically in West Falkland. Photograph **399** shows his grave with the simple cross erected over it by the Argentines.

Acknowledgments

The author is grateful for the chance he has had to enlarge public knowledge of the SAS. He is grateful, first, to the Regiment itself. People of all ranks and every generation of service have given unstinting help, advice and criticism. The Regiment has supplied some of the photographs used in this book. Others, provided anonymously by soldiers who have served or are still serving, are also attributed in this book to the SAS Regiment. In some cases, veterans whom it is possible to identify have made a special contribution to the collection. These include Lieutenant-Colonel Bruce Niven, MBE, MA, whose work ranks him as a photographic artist; the author's friend Nicolas Downie, an SAS veteran turned professional film-maker; David Kirby, the conscript SAS soldier turned architect, who never seems to have moved in the Malayan jungle without his camera, sketch-pad and diary.

Outside the Regiment a number of institutions — notably the Photographic Department of the Imperial War Museum and *Soldier* magazine — have been immensely useful sources for this book. Finally, there are the professional journalists. These include veterans of the trade, such as Terry Fincher and *The Guardian*'s Don McPhee, Hereford's Derek Evans and those equally professional, if anonymous, practitioners whose work bears the imprint of the Press Association, Popperfoto, Camera Press and so on. Finally, there have been those whose laboratory skills have miraculously rejuvenated some fading, geriatric photographs. Ian Hogg, a distinguished military author, was one of them. Another was Michael Dyer Associates of London. To all of them, the author offers his sincere thanks.

Literary Sources

Clutterbuck, Richard, 'Management of the Kidnap Risk' from *British Perspectives on Terrorism* (edited by Paul Wilkinson), Allen and Unwin, London, 1981; quoted on p. 87.
— *Guerrillas and Terrorists*, Faber, London, 1977; quoted on p. 84

Dillon, Martin and Lehane, Denis, *Political Murder in Northern Ireland*, Penguin, London, 1973; quoted on p. 87.

Farran, Roy, *Winged Dagger*, Collins, London, 1948; quoted on p. 28.

Jeapes, Colonel Tony, *SAS: Operation Oman*, William Kimber, London, 1980; quoted on pp. 54 and 70.

Laqueur, Walter, *Terrorism*, Weidenfeld and Nicolson, London, 1977.

Lloyd-Owen, David, *Providence their Guide*, Harrap, London, 1980; quoted on pp. 9 and 18.

Lodwick, John, *The Filibusters*, Methuen, London, 1947; quoted on pp. 8, 9, 20, 21 and 128.

Maclean, Fitzroy, *Eastern Approaches*, Jonathan Cape, London, 1949; quoted on p. 9.

Warner, Philip, *The Special Air Service*, William Kimber, London, 1971; quoted on pp. 9, 14, 55 and 116.

Williams-Hunt, Major P. D. R., *An Introduction to the Malayan Aborigines*, Government Press, Kuala Lumpur, 1952; quoted on p. 41.

Photographic Sources

Associated Press: 235, 236, 384, 385
Australian SAS Regiment: 342, 343, 344, 345, 346, 347, 348
BBC tv/Pilot Press: 382
Bermuda News Bureau: 283
Camera Press: 243, 244 (Colman Doyle); 245 (Don McPhee); 248, 249 (Benoit Gysembergh)
Central Press Photos: 164
Crown Copyright: 396
Daily Express: 231, 233
Daily Telegraph: 144, 145, 146, 148, 153
Devon News Service: 386
Downie, Nick: 240, 242, 278, 279, 295, 296, 297
Evans, Derek (Hereford): 319, 320, 322, 331
Frank Spooner Pictures: 227, 368, 369, 370, 380, 381, 392
Imperial War Museum: 5, 18, 20, 21, 25, 27, 28, 29, 30, 31, 32, 35, 38, 39, 40, 41, 43, 44, 45, 46, 50, 51, 52, 53, 54, 55, 56, 57, 58, 59, 60, 61, 62, 63, 74, 75, 76, 77, 78, 79, 84, 88, 89, 90, 92, 93, 95, 98, 101, 102, 103, 104, 136, 137, 138, 140, 141, 143, 155, 157, 160, 257, 315, 332, 333, 334
Kirby, David: 96, 97, 107, 108, 113, 114, 115, 116, 117, 118, 123, 127, 128, 130, 131, 132, 324
Ministry of Defence: 371, 372, 373, 374, 375, 376
New Zealand Army: 349, 350, 351, 352, 353, 354, 355, 356, 357, 358, 359, 360, 361, 362, 363, 364, 365, 366, 367
Niven Bruce: 2, 3, 4, 169, 171, 172, 173, 174, 175, 176, 177, 179, 182, 189, 193, 196, 205, 206, 214
Pacemaker Press: 237, 238, 239
Photographers International (Terry Fincher): 284, 285
Popperfoto: 226
Press Association: 1, 158, 218, 219, 220, 229, 230, 232, 234, 246, 252, 383, 387, 388, 389, 390, 391
Royal Marines: 268, 269, 377, 378, 379
SAS Regimental Archives: 6, 7, 8, 9, 10, 11, 12, 13, 14, 15, 16, 17, 22, 23, 24, 26, 33, 34, 36, 39, 42, 47, 48, 64, 65, 66, 67, 68, 69, 70, 71, 72, 73, 80, 81, 82, 83, 85, 86, 91, 94, 99, 100, 105, 106, 109, 110, 111, 112, 121, 122, 124, 125, 126, 129, 133, 134, 135, 142, 147, 149, 150, 151, 154, 156, 159, 161, 162, 163, 165, 166, 167, 168, 170, 180, 181, 183, 184, 185, 186, 187, 188, 190, 191, 192, 194, 195, 197, 198, 199, 200, 201, 202, 203, 204, 207, 208, 209, 210, 211, 212, 213, 215, 216, 217, 223, 224, 225, 241, 247, 255, 256, 261, 262, 263, 264, 265, 266, 273, 274, 275, 276, 277, 280, 281, 286, 289, 291, 292, 294, 298, 299, 300, 301, 302, 303, 304, 305, 306, 307, 308, 309, 310, 311, 312, 313, 317, 318, 321, 323, 325, 326, 328, 329, 330, 336, 337, 338, 340, 341, 393, 394, 395, 397, 398, 399
Soldier Magazine: 19, 37, 87, 139, 152, 250, 251, 253, 258, 259, 271, 272, 282, 287, 288, 290, 293, 314, 316, 327, 335, 339
Sunday Times: 221 (Frank Herrmann); 254 (Peter Dunn)
Syndication International (Brendan Monks, *Daily Mirror*): 267
UPI: 222
US Navy: 270